PRAY YOUR WAY INTO DIVINE FAVOR

(Exhaustive Edition)

JOHN MILLER

PRAYERDB

**PRAY YOUR WAY
INTO
DIVINE FAVOR**

John Miller

Copyright © 2024 Polycharis Productions, Inc.

All scriptures quotations are taken from the King James Version of the Bible.

CONTENTS

This book is dedicated to Lawrence & Felicia

MILLER'S BOOK CATALOG

John Miller's book catalog can be found on:

HTTPS://WWW.AMAZON.COM/STORES/AUTHOR/
B00NMDON9G/ALLBOOKS

FREE BONUS CHAPTER

FAVOR
FOR
UNMERITED
ASSISTANCE

Thank you for getting this book "Pray Your Way Into Divine Favor" (Exhaustive Edition)

Please note that owning this book qualifies you to receive the accompanying bonus chapter titled *"Favor for Unmerited Assistance"* for free.

SEE THE LAST PAGE FOR THE DOWNLOAD LINK

PART I
INTRODUCTION

CHAPTER I

WHAT IS DIVINE FAVOR?

Let's take a look at two scriptures that effectively illustrate the phenomenon of Divine Favor:

Proverbs 16:7 (KJV) *"When a man's ways please the LORD, he maketh even his enemies to be at peace with him."*

Acts 7:10 (KJV) *"And delivered him (Joseph) out of all his afflictions, and gave him favour and wisdom in the sight of Pharaoh king of Egypt; and he made him governor over Egypt and all his house."*

These scriptures reveal to us at least two benefits of favor:

a) Favor for the resolution of a serious problem:

Having an enemy is a problem. The potential consequences are wide-ranging and far-reaching. An enemy can cause you to lose a profitable position or situation. He could irreparably damage your reputation, which could then block all progress. Or worse, he could get you killed. So, if you have an enemy, you should be glad that—insofar as you can meet certain conditions—God has put in place a phenomenon that can nullify all the potential dangers that you might otherwise have to contend with.

b) Favor for unbelievable change of circumstance:

Joseph was fortunate to escape being killed by his own brothers. He was pulled out of a pit and sold into slavery. He became a complete nobody. Then, he was put in prison for more than a decade. By any human measure, this was a hopeless man and another failed destiny. However, as Acts 7:10 reveals, Joseph experienced a dramatic change of circumstance and became manager of Pharaoh's house and ruler of the greatest nation on the earth at the time. So, if you believe that your current circumstance is hopeless, hopefully, you can see that you are actually a candidate for divine favor.

From these two examples, we can provide a proper definition for this book's central theme: Divine Favor is a spiritual phenomenon—that is activated, provided and maintained by God—which causes the manifestation of both expected and unexpected breakthroughs in the lives of people who are able to meet certain conditions as stated in the scriptures.

Stages of Divine Favor

Divine Favor has levels or stages as revealed in the following scriptures:

i) Finding Favor

*Genesis 6:8 (KJV) "But Noah **found grace** in the eyes of the LORD."*

ii) Being in Favor

*1 Samuel 2:26 (KJV) "And the child Samuel grew on, and **was in favour** both with the LORD, and also with men."*

iii) Increasing in Favor

Luke 2:52 (KJV) "And Jesus increased in wisdom and stature, and in favour with God and man."

As you will see throughout this book, the benefits that divine favor can confer on your life are infinite. However, to secure your access to these benefits, you first have to *find favor* with God as Noah did. Then, like the prophet Samuel, as soon as you are *in favor* with the Almighty, you will begin to experience His divine benefits. And, as you *increase in favor* with God as the Lord Jesus Christ did, you will witness an explosion of the diverse manifestations of God's favor in your life.

Purpose of this Book

The first purpose of this book is to teach you how exactly you can ask God for His divine favor. Next, you will learn the various requirements you need to meet—as stated in scripture —to find favor with God and increase in it. Finally, this book provides you with diverse manifestations of divine favor that are possible for a human to enjoy, with each manifestation accompanied with the set of prayers you need for approaching Almighty God to request their expression in your own life.

This book contains a lot of information that can change your life dramatically for the best. Read it with all your heart. Consistently do whatever the scriptures tell you to do and wait on God for the manifestation.

God bless you.

PART II
HOW TO ASK FOR DIVINE FAVOR

CHAPTER 2

ACKNOWLEDGE THE SOURCE OF DIVINE FAVOR

"Many seek the ruler's favour; but every man's judgment cometh from the LORD."
— Proverbs 29:26 (KJV)

This verse is actually a continuation of the one preceding it, and the one preceding it is as follows:

Proverbs 29:25 (KJV) *"The fear of man bringeth a snare: but whoso putteth his trust in the LORD shall be safe."*

"Fear of man" here refers to over-dependence on a person or displaying over-reverence for a person in order to get some kind of benefit from that person. Contrary to expectation, having such a fear for a human being may put one in harm's way. An unethical person who detects over-dependence or over-reverence in another person, is likely to ask him or her to do anything, which could possibly lead to any kind of deleterious consequence. No normal person wants this kind of outcome. So, if you have a need, what should you do instead?

According to this scripture, you should put your trust in the Lord, who can grant your request without causing you harm.

Hopefully, you can now better understand our opening scripture.

In this case, the stakes are higher. We are dealing with not just any man BUT a ruler, like a governor or a president or a king or a company leader or some other major leader. Every ruler always has people waiting to see him or her on a daily basis. What are the people there for? They mostly want that ruler's favor for one thing or the other. But, as you can imagine, many requests made to a ruler are either rejected or left pending indefinitely. Only a few requests receive favor and are approved.

So, if you have a request before a ruler or any other person, and you want to be part of the few who are favored, what should you do? The answer lies in the second part of our opening scripture which says "...*every man's judgment cometh from the LORD*". What does this mean? A request before a ruler for a favorable decision is actually a request for a favorable *judgment*. Denying or approving a request is a judgment on the part of that ruler. The ruler considers the request and "makes the decision" or so he or she thinks. The reality is that whatever decision the ruler makes actually comes from Almighty God, acting through him or her.

Therefore, if you want a favorable outcome on any matter, once you have done what is considered as the best possible, instead of committing a sin in order to further enhance your prospects of securing the favor of the person in charge, it is better for you to seek the favor of the Lord who judges all matters including the one you need help with. This means that acknowledging Almighty God as the source of all judgments and all favor is the first step in getting divine favor.

PRAYERS

1. Righteous Father, once again, I am before You to pour out my heart to you. Honor my prayers today and answer them, in the name of Jesus.

2. Father, forgive me for all the times in my life when I have been over-dependent on any person, in the name of Jesus.

3. Lord, forgive me for all the times I have been over-reverent toward any person, in the name of Jesus.

4. Merciful God, forgive me for any sin I may have committed in trying to get the favor of any person, in the name of Jesus.

5. My God, because of my over-dependence on man, I have suffered _____ (mention the consequence). Have mercy, O Lord and deliver me from _____ (consequence), in the name of Jesus.

6. Jehovah, Your word says that anyone who puts their trust in You shall be safe. From today, I declare that You are the only one that I trust absolutely. Now and until the end, I shall trust no one else more than I trust You, in the name of Jesus.

7. O my God, because my trust is in You, according to Your word, keep me safe from the storms of life, in the name of Jesus.

8. My Shepherd, Your word says that every man's judgment in this life comes from you. Based on this revelation, today, I declare that I acknowledge You as the source of all judgments, in the name of Jesus.

9. Lord, I declare that I also acknowledge You as the source of all favors on the earth, in the name of Jesus.

10. Father, from today, whenever I need a favorable response to any request I desire to put before any person, I will present my request to You first, in the knowledge that all favor is from You and favor from You is favor for me before any person, in the name of Jesus.

11. Be merciful unto me, O God. Let me always find favor before You on the important issues of my life, in the name of Jesus.

12. Thank You Father for today's revelation and for answering my prayers, in Jesus' mighty name, amen.

CHAPTER 3

PRAYER IS THE TOOL FOR ASKING FOR FAVOR

"He shall pray unto God, and he will be favourable unto him: and he shall see his face with joy: for he will render unto man his righteousness." — Job 33:26 (KJV)

During Job's period of tribulation, he was visited by a young but spiritual friend named Elihu. Elihu had heard of Job's bitter complaints about the state of his health and so he came to try to set Job straight. At a point during his speech to Job, Elihu began talking about the different manifestations of sickness — about loss of appetite, weight loss, bone pain — up until when a sick person is at the brink of death. However, at this point, Elihu's speech takes a positive turn and he says the following:

Job 33:23-25 (KJV) *"If there be a messenger with him (the dying person), an interpreter, one among a thousand, to shew unto man his uprightness: Then he is gracious unto him, and saith [to God], Deliver him from going down to the pit: I have found a ransom. His flesh shall be fresher than a child's: he shall return to the days of his youth"*

Job 33:26,28 (KJV) *"He shall pray unto God, and **he will be favourable unto him**: and he shall see his face with joy: for he will render unto man his righteousness... He will deliver his soul from going into the pit, and his life shall see the light."*

These are powerful words, especially considering the fact that they are from the old testament. What Elihu was saying in essence is this: A person that is so sick as to be on the brink of dying does not necessarily have to die, as long as he or she has access to a messenger or an interpreter who can mediate between God and the person. As far as this messenger can speak to God on the person's behalf, he or she would have the opportunity to recover.

However, the sick person must seize this opportunity by *praying to God* concerning his situation. And, only then, will God *favor him* and ultimately deliver his soul from going into the pit. What wonderful information!

The only messenger or interpreter or mediator who has the authority to be gracious unto a human being and to tell God to deliver a person from death [because he has a ransom] is Jesus Christ! Therefore, in order for you to get God's favor, you MUST have Jesus with you. And the only way for Him to be with you is to give your life to him. Once you have done this, you will have the right to ask Almighty God for His favor concerning any matter [including recovery from sickness] through prayer.

PRAYERS

1. Most High God, I thank You for letting me realize today that prayer is the tool I can use to ask You for divine favor. To You be all the glory, in the name of Jesus.

2. Again Lord, I thank You for letting me learn that Jesus has to be with me before I can ask You for favor through prayer. Be thou glorified, in the name of Jesus.

3. Now Lord, I declare that I am ready to rededicate my life to Jesus so that He can be with me, in the name of Jesus.

4. Lord Jesus, I _____ (your name) believe that You are the Son of Almighty God sent to this world to die for my sins and by so doing, redeem me from sin, death and hell. I ask You to come into my life and be with me all the days of my life and forever, in the name of Jesus.

5. Lord Jesus, I need divine favor in my life. Come and be the divine **messenger** between me and the Father, in the name of Jesus.

6. Lord Jesus, I need divine favor. Come and be the divine **interpreter** between me and the Father, in the name of Jesus.

7. Lord Jesus, I need divine favor. Come and be the **mediator** between me and Father God, in the name of Jesus.

8. Emmanuel, I ask, according to the word of today, be gracious unto me so that I can become a candidate of divine favor, in the name of Jesus.

9. Messiah, I ask, according to the word of today, through the ransom You have found for me, let me become a candidate of divine favor, in the name of Jesus.

10. My Father, through the intercessory work of Jesus, whenever I open my mouth in prayer, according to the word of today, be favorable unto me, in the name of Jesus.

11. Father God, according to the intercessory work of Jesus, let You favor upon me lead to the resolution of my requests, in the name of Jesus.

12. Thank You O God for answering my prayers, in Jesus' mighty name, amen.

CHAPTER 4

USE YOUR WHOLE HEART FOR BEST RESULTS

"I intreated thy favour with my whole heart..."
— Psalm 119:58a (KJV)

As we saw in our introduction, Divine Favor is a spiritual phenomenon. It is not a common thing. Anyone can get it but God will not give it to everyone. Only very few people who are born into this world will enjoy it. Only people adjudged by God to be serious about it will ever experience divine favor.

The word 'intreat' from our opening scripture is the old form of 'entreat'. It means to 'ask earnestly' or repeatedly for something. In this case, it means to ask God earnestly and repeatedly for divine favor with your whole heart. But what does it mean to intreat God for favor with your whole heart? Let's see a guide for doing this from scripture:

Matthew 6:24a (KJV) *"No man can serve two masters: for either he will hate the one, and love the other; or else he will hold to the one, and despise the other..."*

The masters Jesus was referring to in this instance are God and mammon or money. Anyone who tries to serve both at the same time is likely to end up becoming a slave to money. But if you choose to serve God exclusively, He will give you everything you need including the money.

In the same manner, asking God earnestly and repeatedly for divine favor requires your total concentration. You have to avoid all distractions during the period you have set aside for asking God for this uncommon blessing. You cannot be in a session of prayer wherein you are asking for something as serious and life-changing as divine favor and then you are also thinking about checking your email or watching your favorite TV show or going to the mall or paying your bills or whatever. No. You would just be wasting your time. Divine favor requires you to use your whole heart, otherwise you get nothing.

If you look at the chapter wherein our opening scripture is situated, you will notice that the verses that precede it enumerate the attributes of the author (most likely David) of the psalm. Here are a few examples of the psalm author's attributes in relation to his entreatment of God for divine favor.

i) He was not ashamed of his relationship with God. v6

ii) He praised God with uprightness of heart. v7

iii) He kept God's statutes. v8

iv) He hid God's word in his heart, so he wouldn't sin against Him. v11

v) He derived happiness from God's word. v16

...and so on. It is only a person as profound as this or better than this who can confidently approach God for favor with his or her whole heart. So as you get ready to seek the face of God for divine favor using this book, are you publicly proud of your relationship with God? Do you keep God's statutes? Have you hid His word in your heart? Do scriptures genuinely make you happy? Can you hold a prayer session for a good period of time while thinking of nothing else but the Lord? Only if you can honestly say yes to these questions will you be ready to use your whole heart to request for divine favor.

PRAYERS

1. Jehovah God, I understand for a fact that divine favor is a spiritual phenomenon and therefore an uncommon blessing. Yet, I desire it. Have mercy on me and let me get it, in the name of Jesus.

2. Omnipotent God, I know that while anyone can get divine favor, You will not give it to everyone. Yet I want it in my life. Be gracious unto me and let me have it in my life, in the name of Jesus.

3. Rock of Ages, even though only very few people who are born into this world will enjoy divine favor, I ask today that I should be one of the few, in the name of Jesus.

4. O Father, it is true that only people You adjudge to be serious about divine favor will ever experience it. Be merciful unto me and make me serious enough to merit the blessing of divine favor in my life, in the name of Jesus.

5. I declare unto You Father that I am willing to ask You earnestly for the blessing of Your divine favor. Give ear to my prayers and answer me, in the name of Jesus.

6. Holy Father, I am willing to ask you repeatedly for the blessing of divine favor until You are satisfied that I merit it.

Be merciful and honor my prayers, in the name of Jesus.

7. Righteous Father, I live in a generation where there are so many distractions. I know that if I am to secure divine favor in my life, I must ask for it with my whole heart. So, I ask: give me the grace to seek Your face without succumbing to the distractions around me, in the name of Jesus.

8. Lord, give me the grace to not succumb to the distractions within me, in the name of Jesus.

9. O God, let Your word that I have hidden deep within my heart keep me completely grounded in prayer as I seek Your face for divine favor, in the name of Jesus.

10. Like the psalmist, my God, let the happiness that I derive from the scriptures keep me focused in the place of prayer until I achieve the desire of my heart, in the name of Jesus.

11. My God, let me be profound enough in my relationship with You so that it is clear that I am indeed a candidate of Your divine favor, in the name of Jesus.

12. Now Lord, by reason of my entreatment, let me enjoy divine favor in my life, in the name of Jesus.

13. Almighty, by reason of my complete focus and the use of my whole heart in asking for Your favor, let me receive it, in the name of Jesus.

14. I am not in this world to waste my life. I am here to maximize the fulfillment of my destiny. And if divine favor is necessary for the fulfillment of my destiny, I shall possess it, in the name of Jesus.

15. Thank You Almighty God for answering my prayers, in Jesus' mighty name, amen.

CHAPTER 5

DIVINE FAVOR PRAYER
TEMPLATE

**"Make thy face to shine upon thy servant: save me for
thy mercies' sake." — Psalm 31:16 (KJV)**

One of the reasons why many Jews did not believe in Jesus
during his earthly ministry was because, most of the time, to
them, he looked like any other human being. They knew his
father, mother and siblings. They watched Him grow up. In
Mark 6:3, we are told that he was in fact a carpenter before his
ministry began. This means that people came to him with
projects. He negotiated prices with customers. He went to the
market. He bought wood and other carpentry supplies, etc. So,
for many, it would have been quite tough to believe the things
he was telling them. However, what people publicly saw was
not even up to a millionth of who Jesus Christ actually was.

One day, after his ministry had began, he took three of his
disciples—Peter, James and John—and they climbed up into a

high mountain, where there were no other people, and the following happened:

Matthew 17:2, (KJV) *"And [He] was transfigured before them: and his face did shine as the sun, and his raiment was white as the light... And as they came down from the mountain, Jesus charged them, saying, Tell the vision to no man, until the Son of man be risen again from the dead."*

This was the real Jesus.

This event has a lot of perspectives to it. But for our purposes here, we will focus on the perspective of Peter, James and John. Throughout the gospels, there are verses that emphasize Jesus going to pray in the night or going into a mountain by Himself, etc. The event we just examined was basically what happened at each of those private sessions. Jesus would transform into a glorified being and emissaries from heaven—angels or saints of old or other such beings—would appear to Him and engage Him in conversation.

These are not sessions that regular people can experience regularly. Therefore, when Jesus' face lit up and shone like the sun, it was because Peter, James and John were favored by Him. He knew the thoughts of their hearts. He knew how righteous they were. He caused His face to shine in their presence because—based on what He could see per their hearts— they had won his favor. Hence the privilege of witnessing the event.

Psalm 31, from which we have taken our opening scripture, is a psalm of deliverance. It was written by David most likely at the time he was being pursued by Saul. In one of the verses, David goes straight to the point:

Psalm 31:9a (KJV) *"Have mercy upon me, O Lord, for I am in trouble..."*

And it is this trouble that brings us to our opening scripture. The shining face of Jesus before Peter, James and John means *"I know you"*, *"I am satisfied with the thoughts and imaginations of your heart"*, *"You are important to me"*, *"You have found favor with me"*.

David understood that if the Almighty could make His face shine upon him, all the troubles he was facing would be over. Of all the zillions upon zillions of things going on in the universe and in heaven, for the creator of the universe to actually turn to a person and cause His face to shine on that person, it means that, He is satisfied with that person, the person is important to Him and that the person has found favor with Him. And therefore, whatever they were going through would be resolved quickly.

So, with this, David has provided you with a prayer template that you can use if you need Divine Favor.

"Have mercy upon me, O Lord, for I am in trouble..."

"Make thy face to shine upon thy servant: save me for thy mercies' sake."

David's prayer template appears to be quite simple. You state the reality of your situation to God and then you ask for His face to shine upon you. Meaning, God should favor you and help you resolve your problem, need or desire. But you have to remember that for this prayer to work for you, you have to be like David or Peter or James or John. That is, a person whose thoughts and imaginations are satisfactory before God and who is therefore known by God and important to Him.

PRAYERS

1. O my Father, I want to experience divine favor in the same manner that Peter, James and John did. Give ear to my prayers today and answer me, in the name of Jesus.

2. My God, I want to have the same audacity that David had to request for Your divine favor. Have mercy upon me and answer my prayers, in the name of Jesus.

3. O Lord my Lamp, I recognize that experiencing divine favor requires me to be an uncommon human being. Come to my aid so that I can become uncommon for good, in the name of Jesus.

4. My Father and my God, you can see my heart and you know how it needs to be before I can access Your divine favor. Purge my heart with the Blood of Jesus until my thoughts and my imaginations are acceptable to You, in the name of Jesus.

5. Father, in the same manner in which Jesus Christ knew and acknowledged Peter, James and John, let me become known and acknowledged for good in heaven, in the name of Jesus.

6. O Righteous Father, in the same manner, Peter, James and John were important to Jesus, let me become important to You, in the name of Jesus.

7. Messiah, in the same manner Peter, James and John found favor before Jesus to be selected for an uncommon experience, let me also find favor before You for uncommon experiences, in the name of Jesus.

8. Alpha, David called out to You in his time of trouble and You heard him. I am calling out to You now in my time of need. Hear me and answer me, in the name of Jesus.

9. Omega, David asked that You make Your face shine upon him and You answered him. I am calling out to You now to also make Your face shine upon me. Be merciful and answer me, in the name of Jesus.

10. Keep me, O Lord, in the path of righteousness so that my privileged access to You can be sustained, in the name of Jesus.

11. I bless You O Lord for the privilege of saying these prayers and for the privilege of Your answers.

12. Thank You Mighty God for answering my prayers, in Jesus' mighty name, amen.

PART III
REQUIREMENTS FOR OBTAINING DIVINE FAVOR

CHAPTER 6

GOD MUST KNOW YOU BY NAME

"And the LORD said unto Moses, I will do this thing also that thou hast spoken: for thou hast found grace in my sight, and I know thee by name."
— Exodus 33:17 (KJV)

In Exodus 33, God told Moses to depart—with all the Israelites—from the base of Mount Sinai and to start heading toward the promised land. However, because of their idolatrous worship of the golden calf, God said that He would not go with the Israelites as He had done up until that point.

But, without God's presence, what laid ahead for the Israelites in the desert was hunger, thirst, disease and possible annihilation by the hand of intolerant kingdoms. Moses must have realized all of these and quickly protested the Almighty's decision. Let's find out how he did this from scripture:

Exodus 33:13-16 (KJV) *"Now therefore, I pray thee, if I have found grace in thy sight, shew me now thy way, that I may know thee,* *that I may find grace in thy sight: and consider that this nation is thy people. And he (God) said, My presence shall go with thee, and I will give thee rest. And he (Moses) said unto him (God),* **If thy presence go not with me, carry us not up hence**. *For wherein shall it be known here that I and thy people have found grace in thy sight? is it not in that thou goest with us? so shall we be separated, I and thy people, from all the people that are upon the face of the earth."*

The phrase "to find grace in Your sight" as used by Moses in the foregoing scripture essentially means "to be favored" by God. Moses is telling God here that without Your presence, there's no point leaving this base of Mount Sinai. Further, You have said that we are Your chosen people, your favored people. But if You are not in our midst, leading us through the wilderness en route the promised land, it means we, as a people, do not have Your divine favor. Can you imagine a human being having a conversation like this with the Creator of the universe? Imagine yourself having such a conversation. It's mind-blowing.

So, how did God respond to Moses' request or holy protest? It's already stated in our opening scripture but let's re-state it again for emphasis:

Exodus 33:17 (KJV) *"And the LORD said unto Moses, I will do this thing also that thou hast spoken: for thou hast found grace in my sight, and I know thee by name."*

God granted Moses' request and decided to go with the Israelites, why? Because Moses had found grace in His sight. That is, Moses had divine favor.

Not only that, God also granted Moses' request because He *"knew Moses by name"*. What does this mean? You see God knows everyone and everything. He even knows the number of the strands of hair on the heads of all humans ever created from their birth till their death. So, He knows everyone. BUT to know Moses by name means that He had a special and uncommon relationship with Moses that he did not have with other people. And this is why he honored Moses' request and agreed to go with Israel on their journey home.

If you want divine favor operational in your life, an intelligent question to ask would then be *"Why did God know Moses by name?"* The answer lies in these scriptures:

Numbers 12:3 (KJV) *"Now the man **Moses was very meek**, above all the men which were upon the face of the earth."*

Exodus 2:11a (KJV) *"And it came to pass in those days, when Moses was grown, that he went out unto his brethren, and **looked on their burdens**..."*

Hebrews 11:24-25 (KJV) *"By faith Moses, when he was come to years, refused to be called the son of Pharaoh's daughter; Choosing rather to suffer affliction with the people of God, than to enjoy the pleasures of sin for a season"*

Moses was a meek man. He was a caring man despite his privileged upbringing in a palace. He set aside his luxurious life because the whole thing was built upon idolatry and sin. These attributes are part of the reason why God knew Moses by name and had a special relationship with him, thus making him a beneficiary of divine favor to the end that whenever he called, the Almighty answered.

PRAYERS

1. According to the words of Moses, Father, show me now Your way, in the name of Jesus.

2. According to the words of Moses, O Lord, let me know You, in the name of Jesus.

3. According to the words of Moses, My God, let me find grace in Your sight, in the name of Jesus.

4. Almighty God, whether I go to or fro, have mercy and let Your presence always go with me, in the name of Jesus.

5. Holy Father, let Your mark of divine distinction be placed upon me even in this generation, in the name of Jesus.

6. El Shaddai, Moses was meek and because of this, You knew him by name. Let that same trait of meekness which was upon Moses fall upon my life now, in the name of Jesus.

7. Redeemer, Moses was a caring man who was concerned with the welfare of his people and for this, You knew him by name. Let that same caring nature and burden for the welfare of others that was upon Moses enter into my life now, in the name of Jesus.

8. King of kings, Moses chose to set aside a life of luxury because it was built on idolatry and sin, and for this, You knew him by name. let that same sacrificial nature which was upon Moses enter into my life now, in the name of Jesus.

9. Lord of Lords, have mercy and know me by my name today, in the name of Jesus.

10. Great King, have mercy and as it was with Moses, let me have a special relationship with You, in the name of Jesus.

11. Almighty God, as it was with Moses, let me also find grace in Your sight, in the name of Jesus.

12. Messiah, as it was with Moses, let me experience Your divine favor, in the name of Jesus.

13. Jehovah God, by reason of Your favor upon my life, let it be that when I make an important request, as it was with Moses, You shall do that which I have spoken, for my benefit and for Your glory, in the name of Jesus.

14. Thank You Mighty God for answering my prayers, in Jesus' mighty name, amen.

CHAPTER 7

FAVOR DUE TO LIVING A LIFE PLEASING TO GOD

"And he that sent me is with me: the Father hath not left me alone; for I do always those things that please him." — John 8:29 (KJV)

Jesus got into quite a number of back and forth encounters with the scribes and Pharisees. Many of these encounters were triggered by the Pharisees with the aim of getting Jesus to say something contrary to what was in the law, which would then give them the right to bring Him down.

One morning in a temple located in the mount of Olives, they dragged a woman caught in the act of adultery before Him, reminding Him that the position of the law regarding the woman was that she had to be stoned. But, they wanted Him to state His own opinion of what should happen to the woman. This was a trap. To this Jesus replied that the first person that should stone the woman should be whomever amongst them who was without any sin in his life... They all left the temple. What an embarrassment! Sinner Pharisees wanted to kill another sinner! But they had been found out by the omniscient Christ!

On that same day, the Pharisees were at it again with Jesus, asking all sorts of questions designed to trap Him. He began telling them things they had never heard before. For instance, He said that He was 'the light of the world'. He said that they would all die in their sins, that they were from beneath and that He was from above and so on. Ordinarily speaking, because He was saying all of these things in a temple, He would have been arrested. But, he wasn't. Why? Let's find out from scriptures:

John 8:20 (KJV) *"These words spake Jesus in the treasury, as he taught in the temple: and no man laid hands on him; for his hour was not yet come."*

Since his time to lay down his life had not come, no man could touch him! Hallelujah! There was a restraining presence with Jesus throughout his earthly ministry that protected Him against all harm. But what was powering this presence? Jesus provides the answer to this in the same John 8. This power is described in our opening scripture but we will re-state it again here for emphasis:

John 8:29 (KJV) *"And he that sent me is with me: the Father hath not left me alone; for I do always those things that please him."*

The thing powering the protection of Jesus Christ was the divine favor of His Father. *"He that sent me is with me"*. When God is with someone, it means that person is enjoying His divine favor. And why did Jesus continue to enjoy this divine favor? According to Him *"for I do always those things that please him."*

Herein lies a great requirement for obtaining divine favor from Almighty God. You must 'always do' those things that please Him. The question now is how do you know those things that please God the Father. Here's your answer, again supplied by the Lord Jesus Christ:

John 15:10 (KJV) *"If ye keep my commandments, ye shall abide in my love; even as I have kept my Father's commandments, and abide in his love."*

So, the way for you to discover those things that please God the Father is to find out all the commandments of Jesus. A simple internet search will show you all of Christ's commands. Once you have found them, begin to always do them. Your persistence in doing them will qualify you for the uncommon blessing of divine favor.

PRAYERS

1. Most High God, give me a heart that thirsts for and longs for Your commands, in the name of Jesus.

2. Everlasting Father, give me a heart of obedience to You, in the name of Jesus.

3. Eternal King, like Jesus, let me find pleasure in always doing what pleases You, in the name of Jesus.

4. King of kings, let me always find pleasure in always keeping the commandments of Jesus, in the name of Jesus.

5. Lord of Lords, as I learn them, let the text of Christ's commandments be installed deep in my soul so that I can never forget them, in the name of Jesus.

6. Yahweh, bless me with the zeal to see each new day as an opportunity to implement the commands of Christ, in the name of Jesus.

7. My God, as I live in obedience and do what pleases You, let me abide in the love of Christ, in the name of Jesus.

8. As it was for Jesus, as I live in obedience, O God, come and be with me, in the name of Jesus.

9. Holy One of Israel, as it was with Jesus, as I live in obedience, do not leave me alone in this world, in the name of Jesus.

10. I Am that I Am, by reason of Your presence in my life, let me enjoy Your manifest divine favor, in the name of Jesus.

11. In the same manner Jesus experienced the benefits of divine favor including divine protection, Holy Father, let me also experience the benefits of divine favor for the rest of my life, in the name of Jesus.

12. Thank You Excellency for answering my prayers, in Jesus' mighty name, amen.

CHAPTER 8

FAVOR DUE TO GENERATIONAL COVENANTS

"And the LORD was gracious unto them, and had compassion on them, and had respect unto them, because of his covenant with Abraham, Isaac, and Jacob, and would not destroy them, neither cast he them from his presence as yet." — 2 Kings 13:23 (KJV)

Solomon had 700 princesses as wives and 300 concubines. 700 princesses meant that he married 700 foreigners. Today, intermarriage is not that much of an issue because Christianity is widespread. So, an American believer can marry an African believer and their joint faith in Jesus Christ would keep on the same path of destiny regardless of the difference in race. No problem. However, in Solomon's day, 700 princesses meant 700 foreigners and 700 idol worshipers, at least.

With time, Solomon, the son of a holy man and a person blessed by God Himself with great wisdom, began seeing 'sense' in the various religions of his lovers. He built temples for the worship of some of these idols and his heart began turning away from the Almighty. The consequence was that his family lost control of the united kingdom of Israel with a man named Jeroboam gaining control of 10 tribes.

Jeroboam himself, with time, built temples for idols and made the Israelites in the cities he ruled worship them. Other kings also came into power after Jeroboam and unfortunately, followed his template. However, during the tenure of kings Jehoahaz and Jehoash, as the Israelites persisted in their idol worship, God empowered Hazael king of Syria and his son Benhadad to oppress them very harshly.

It is at this point that we arrive at our opening scripture. You can see from the text of the verse that God could have banished the Israelites completely from His presence or utterly destroyed them BUT there was something preventing Him from doing this. Let's re-state what that was here again for emphasis:

*2 Kings 13:23 (KJV) "And **the LORD was gracious unto them**, and had compassion on them, and had respect unto them, **because of his covenant** with Abraham, Isaac, and Jacob, and would not destroy them, neither cast he them from his presence as yet."*

The covenant that God made with Abraham, Isaac and Jacob 'compelled' the Almighty to be gracious unto them, that is, to favor them and to be compassionate to them and to respect or regard them.

So, here we learn a new lesson, which is that a person or persons can enjoy divine favor by reason of an ancestral covenant. Logically, the next question to ask is: what exactly was this covenant that compelled the Almighty to show the Israelites favor despite their sins?

Let's find out from scripture:

Genesis 17:1-10 (KJV) *"And when Abram was ninety years old and nine, the Lord appeared to Abram, and said unto him, I am the Almighty God; walk before me, and be thou perfect. And I will make my covenant between me and thee, and will multiply thee exceedingly. And Abram fell on his face: and God talked with him, saying, As for me, behold, my covenant is with thee, and thou shalt be a father of many nations. Neither shall thy name any more be called Abram, but thy name shall be Abraham; for a father of many nations have I made thee. And I will make thee exceeding fruitful, and I will make nations of thee, and kings shall come out of thee. And I will establish my covenant between me and thee and thy seed after thee in their generations for an everlasting covenant, to be a God unto thee, and to thy seed after thee. And I will give unto thee, and to thy seed after thee, the land wherein thou art a stranger, all the land of Canaan, for an everlasting possession; and I will be their God. And God said unto Abraham, Thou shalt keep my covenant therefore, thou, and thy seed after thee in their generations. This is my covenant, which ye shall keep, between me and you and thy seed after thee; Every man child among you shall be circumcised."*

In the covenant, amongst other things, God said "*And I will give unto thee, and to thy seed after thee, the land wherein thou art a stranger, all the land of Canaan, for an everlasting possession; and I will be their God*" Therefore, if He banished them from His presence or destroyed them, there would be no Israelite left to occupy Canaan. He would have broken His covenant. But since God magnifies His word above His name, He couldn't. This is why He was compelled to show the Israelites His favor in the form of compassion, regard and preservation of their lives.

You might be asking yourself "*Well, good for the Israelites BUT how does this concern me?*" It concerns you for these reasons:

Genesis 12:3 (KJV) *"And I will bless them that bless thee [Abraham], and curse him that curseth thee: and in thee shall all families of the earth be blessed."*

Galatians 3:17 (KJV) *"Now to Abraham and his seed were the promises made. He saith not, And to seeds, as of many; but as of one, And to thy seed, which is Christ."*

Galatians 3:13-14 (KJV) *"Christ hath redeemed us from the curse of the law, being made a curse for us: for it is written, Cursed is every one that hangeth on a tree: That the blessing of Abraham might come on the Gentiles through Jesus Christ; that we might receive the promise of the Spirit through faith."*

God said that through Abraham, "all the families of the earth" will be blessed. Further, the Apostle Paul said that God's covenant promises to Abraham were to him and his seed. This seed includes ultimately, Jesus Christ, a natural descendant of Abraham. Then, when Jesus was killed on the Cross of Calvary, He, who was a natural descendant of Abraham, then connected all who had faith in Him to the Abrahamic covenant. This connection guarantees that a gentile who believes in Jesus Christ can receive the blessing of Abraham which includes baptism in the Holy Spirit as well as the divine favor the Israelites enjoyed which protected them against divine judgment. Therefore, if you are a believer, divine favor through generational covenants is your portion.

PRAYERS

1. Most High God, I am sorry for any sin I am guilty of. Have mercy and forgive me, in the name of Jesus.

2. By reason of what I have learned today, I boldly declare that I am a descendant of Abraham, in the name of Jesus.

3. Father God, You told Abraham that because of him, all the families of the earth shall be blessed. I am a member of a family on this earth. Therefore, I ask that the blessing of Abraham be released into my life and my family, in the name of Jesus.

4. Eternal King, Your promises were made to Abraham and his seed including Jesus Christ, who died for me. Let the benefits of the death of Jesus be fully realized in my life, in the name of Jesus.

5. Jesus was hung on a tree in Calvary including for the reason that the blessing of Abraham could come on Gentiles. I am a gentile and a believer in Jesus. Lord God, let the blessing of Abraham come on me now, in the name of Jesus.

6. My God, I am a gentile and a believer in Jesus, let the promise of the Spirit be unleashed on me now, in the name of Jesus.

7. Mighty God, I am a gentile and a believer in Jesus, let the same divine favor which the Israelites enjoyed by reason of Your covenant with Abraham, come on me now, in the name of Jesus.

8. By reason of Your divine favor, as it was for the Israelites, Father, be gracious unto me, in the name of Jesus.

9. By reason of Your divine favor, as it was for the Israelites, Almighty, have compassion on me, in the name of Jesus.

10. By reason of Your divine favor, as it was for the Israelites, O Lord, have regard unto me, in the name of Jesus.

11. Lord God of heaven, by reason of Your divine favor, do not banish me or cast me out of Your presence because of my sins, in the name of Jesus.

12. Most High, by reason of Your divine favor, do not destroy me because of my sins, in the name of Jesus.

13. O Lord my God, be merciful unto me. Let any spirit of Hazael or Benhadad dispatched against me in divine judgment, because of my sins, be withdrawn from my life permanently, in the name of Jesus.

14. Let You favor guide me away from iniquity and toward Your light, in the name of Jesus.

15. Thank You Great and Mighty God for answering my prayers, in Jesus' mighty name, amen.

CHAPTER 9

FAVOR DUE TO HAVING GOOD UNDERSTANDING

"Good understanding giveth favour: but the way of transgressors is hard." — Proverbs 13:15 (KJV)

At first glance, the meaning of our opening scripture appears hard to decipher. What does "Good understanding giveth favour" mean? Because the common use of 'understanding' is with respect to academics. That is, it is common for believers who are students to ask God for understanding, so they can better grasp lectures or the contents of their textbooks. But what has that got to do with divine favor?

To decipher the meaning of this verse, it's best to see what another Bible version says. One of them says the following:

Good understanding wins favor

but the way of the faithless is difficult

This makes things much clearer. The second part of the verse, which is supposed to be the opposite of the first part, says that 'the way of the faithless is difficult'. This means that 'good understanding' here has nothing to do with academics but everything to do with faith or spirituality. We are making progress.

There's at least one scripture available to help us have a better insight into our opening scripture and it says the following:

Proverbs 9:10 (KJV) *"The fear of the LORD is the beginning of wisdom: and the knowledge of the holy is understanding."*

Other versions use *"the Holy One"* instead of *"the Holy"*.

Now we have the complete picture.

Proverbs 9:10 says that understanding = knowledge of the Holy One

So, if we substitute the word 'understanding' with 'knowledge of the Holy One' in our opening scripture, we will have the following:

"Good knowledge of the Holy One giveth favour: but the way of transgressors or the faithless is hard."

That's perfect! Our opening scripture now makes a lot of sense.

Anyone who is faithless is a transgressor and his way through life will be hard. On the other hand, anyone who has a good knowledge of the Holy One, that is Almighty God, will experience divine favor in his or her life.

But, how does one get good knowledge of the Holy One in order to get divine favor? Again, let's find out from scripture:

Psalm 111:10 (KJV) *"The fear of the LORD is the beginning of wisdom:* **a good understanding have all they that do his commandments:** *his praise endureth for ever."*

In order to have a good understanding of the Holy One, one has to "do" His commandments.

The Lord's commandments are written in the Bible. There are guides available online or in book form which list out all of God the Father's commandments as well as Christ's commandments. If you master these commandments and do them consistently, you will get good understanding. And with good understanding, you will get divine favor with which you can live an unbelievable life.

PRAYERS

1. I declare that I am not a transgressor. Therefore, may my way in life not be hard, in the name of Jesus.

2. I declare that I am not faithless. Therefore, may my way in life not be difficult, in the name of Jesus.

3. I have the fear of the Lord deep within my heart. Therefore, I also have His wisdom, in the name of Jesus.

4. Now Lord, I want to be an uncommon believer so I can experience all the blessings of the faith. Come to my aid, in the name of Jesus.

5. Father, Your word says that all who do Your commandments have good understanding. Give me an uncommon interest and love for Your word so I can dig deep into it to locate Your commandments, in the name of Jesus.

6. Holy Father, give me an uncommon desire to carry out Your commands all the days of my life, in the name of Jesus.

7. My God, as I do Your commandments, let my knowledge of You begin to grow, in the name of Jesus.

8. Lord, as my knowledge of You grows, let my understanding become wider and deeper, in the name of Jesus.

9. O God, according to Your word, as my good understanding grows, have mercy on me and give me Your favor, in the name of Jesus.

10. Divine Shepherd, with Your favor in my life, let my path through life be easier, in the name of Jesus.

11. Create in me, O God, a heart of humility, so that my knowledge or understanding of You will puff me up and cause my downfall, in the name of Jesus.

12. Thank You Father God for answering my prayers, in Jesus' mighty name, amen.

CHAPTER 10

FAVOR DUE TO BEING A GOOD PERSON

"A good man obtaineth favour of the LORD: but a man of wicked devices will he condemn."
— Proverbs 12:2 (KJV)

Here we are presented with two further requirements to qualify for divine favor.

1. Never become a person of wicked devices

A person of wicked devices is someone who habitually thinks about and / or plans and executes wickedness or evil against others. This can be any kind of evil as far as it will do some kind of damage to others. Examples of wicked devices includes wishing that evil befalls an innocent person, spreading false rumors about others, planning to entrap someone so they can be responsible for something they aren't or convicted of a crime, planning to set someone up for workplace dismissal, making efforts to cause the closure of someone's business, trying to steal someone else's partner or spouse, wishing for or planning to get someone injured or killed, leading a person away from the path of righteousness, derailing a person's destiny, etc.

Anyone who does any of these aforementioned things can never obtain the favor of God.

2. Become a good person

What does it mean to become a good person in the context of our current focus? The first hint of the meaning is derived from our opening scripture. A good person is one who does not device wickedness. Instead, he or she does the opposite. Thus, if you habitually and constantly think about, plan and execute acts of goodness for the benefit of others, within our context here, you are a good person.

The Bible provides us with more insight into what it means to be a good person as follows:

Psalm 112:5 (KJV) *"A good man sheweth favour, and lendeth: he will guide his affairs with discretion."*

Hebrews 13:16 (KJV) *"But to do good and to communicate forget not: for with such sacrifices God is well pleased."*

Isaiah 1:17 (KJV) *"Learn to do well; seek judgment, relieve the oppressed, judge the fatherless, plead for the widow."*

The first aforementioned scripture is fairly straightforward. It says that a good man [or woman] is one who shows favor [unto other people] especially through the act of lending. So as long as you habitually lend out money or any item you have in your possession or your time, according to this scripture, you are a good person.

The meaning of the second aforementioned scripture may not be immediately apparent. It says "... *to do good and to communicate forget not...*" That is, do good especially by 'communicating'. What does this mean? The word "communicate" here means to "share". So, when re-phrased, the scripture is saying "Do good by sharing". In the previous scripture, the emphasis was on lending, here, it is on sharing. So, if you have money or other items in excess, sharing them to those who need them demonstrates that—in the context of our study focus—you are a good man or woman.

The final scripture provides multiple examples of what it means to do good:

i) Seek Judgment: meaning, in any case between two people, be fair.

ii) Relieve the oppressed: meaning, do 'as much as you can' to end the oppression in the lives of others, especially believers [Galatians 6:10].

iii) Judge the fatherless: meaning, have a special place in your heart for the fatherless, and treat them with above-average consideration, especially those who are believers.

iv) Plead for the window: meaning, assist widows as much as you can, especially those who are believers.

All of the foregoing is what it means to be a good person. If you habitually practice these things, in time, heaven will take notice, and according to the Word of God, you will obtain the favor of the Lord and all its life-changing benefits.

PRAYERS

1. Everlasting Father, Your favor in my life will guarantee the acceleration of my destiny. Therefore, I am prepared to do all

that is necessary to get it. Have mercy on me and answer my prayers in this session, in the name of Jesus.

2. Lord, I know that You abhor any man or woman of wicked devices. Therefore, if there be any time in my life in which I have been a person of wicked devices, forgive me, in the name of Jesus.

3. My Father, I repent of any negative thought I have had toward any innocent person. Forgive me, in the name of Jesus.

4. My God, I repent of any plan of wickedness I have ever made against any innocent person. Forgive me, in the name of Jesus.

5. Jehovah, I repent of any act of evil I have ever carried out against any innocent person. Forgive me, in the name of Jesus.

6. Messiah, I ask that You take control of my heart and cleanse it so that I can never return to wicked devices, in the name of Jesus.

7. Rock of Ages, it is my intention to impress You throughout my life. If doing good will impress You. I am here for it. Come to my aid, in the name of Jesus.

8. Lord, give me the grace to constantly think about doing good to others, in the name of Jesus.

9. Great King, give me the grace to habitually plan to do good for others, in the name of Jesus.

10. Eternal King, give me the grace—mentally, spiritually and physically—to habitually execute all the good plans I have for people, in the name of Jesus.

11. From today, I will consciously show people favor by lending my money or whatever else I have available to lend, and my time. Help me O Lord, in the name of Jesus.

12. From today, I will plan to and actually share whatever I have in excess for the benefit of others, in the name of Jesus.

13. Heavenly Father, give me the grace to always be fair whenever I am called upon to judge a matter between people, in the name of Jesus.

14. El Shaddai, give me the grace to do as much as I can to relieve oppression in the lives of others, especially believers like me, in the name of Jesus.

15. Holy One of Israel, give me the grace to develop and maintain a special place in my heart for the fatherless, and to treat them with kind consideration, especially those who are believers like me, in the name of Jesus.

16. Jehovah God, give me the grace to assist widows as much as I can, especially those who are believers like me, in the name of Jesus.

17. Lord, as I begin to do these good things I have enumerated, according to Your word, let Your face shine upon me and let me receive Your divine favor, in the name of Jesus.

18. Thank You Great God for answering my prayers, in Jesus' mighty name, amen.

CHAPTER 11

FAVOR DUE TO DOING THINGS THE CORRECT WAY

"And Abel, he also brought of the firstlings of his flock and of the fat thereof. And the LORD had respect unto Abel and to his offering" — Genesis 4:4 (KJV)

Two brothers—Cain and Abel—brought offerings to the Lord. Cain was the elder, Abel was the younger. God "had respect" or looked favorably at Abel's offering. However, unto Cain's offering, he neither respected nor looked at with favor. Why? What did Abel do that caused him to win God's favor and what did Cain not do that caused him to reap disfavor?

Here are two passages from scripture that provide more insight as to why:

Genesis 4:6-7a (KJV) *"And the Lord said unto Cain, Why art thou wroth? and why is thy countenance fallen? If thou doest well, shalt thou not be accepted? ..."*

Hebrews 11:4 (KJV) *"By faith Abel offered unto God a more excellent sacrifice than Cain, by which he obtained witness that he was righteous, God testifying of his gifts..."*

When Cain realized that his offering did not receive God's favor, he got angry. So, the Lord paid him a visit and told him that the reason his offering was not respected was because he did not "do well". In other words, he did not do the right thing or the correct thing. Further, Hebrews 11:4 reveals that Abel got favor because he offered a "more excellent sacrifice" than Cain. So, when God told Cain that he did not do the correct thing, He meant that Cain presented the wrong or an inferior sacrifice.

Let's take a quick look again at the sacrifices of both brothers:

"Cain brought of ***the fruit of the ground*** *an offering unto the Lord" Genesis 4:3 (KJV)*

"And Abel, he also brought of the firstlings of his flock and of the fat thereof" Genesis 4:4 (KJV)

As you can imagine, there are various "interpretations" of what happened in this Biblical case. But, we have to go with what is written in the Word of God.

So, we've seen both sacrifices. What are the differences?

Let's start with Abel's. Clearly you can see that Abel's approach was more thorough. He selected the 'firstlings' or firstborns of his sheep, which he then had to kill. So, the sacrifice involved blood, which is the life of the animal and which, in that era, added more spiritual weight to the sacrifice. Then, from those animals, he extracted the "fat" or the choicest parts, which he then offered to the Almighty. This shows that

Abel was very considerate and very respectful of the Almighty. He presented only the best of the best.

As for Cain, you can see that there wasn't much planning or much thought to his sacrifice. He just picked some crops from his field and presented them to the Lord. Minimal effort. Not much thought or consideration.

Look at these two approaches. Be honest, if you were God, whose sacrifice would you respect or favor? It has to be Abel's!

So, we are shown a new lesson here, which is that; when it comes to obtaining divine favor from God, it's not about just doing what is right but about doing what is right the correct or proper way. Yes, Cain did the right thing by presenting a sacrifice to the Lord. However, as the scriptures reveal, he did not do it well. His sacrifice was not considered to be excellent. Therefore, no favor. Cain also did the right thing BUT he did it in the correct way. He did it excellently. Therefore, favor.

Here's a similar situation:

Matthew 6:1 (KJV) *"Take heed that ye do not your alms before men, to be seen of them: otherwise ye have no reward of your Father which is in heaven."*

It is good to give alms or to be charitable, and it does come with rewards from the Lord. However, if you give alms to show off, you will get no reward from Him.

Do the right thing well, in the correct way and the Lord will give you His divine favor.

PRAYERS

1. Father, I need Your divine favor to power me through life. Give ear to my prayers in this session and answer them, in the name of Jesus.

2. Any spirit of Cain in my life, I bind you with fetters of fire that can never be broken and I command you: Depart from my life now and never return, in the name of Jesus.

3. Any spirit of *inferior* sacrifices toward God in my life, depart and never return, in the name of Jesus.

4. Any spirit of *wrong* sacrifices toward God in my life, depart and never return, in the name of Jesus.

5. Any spirit of minimal effort toward the things of God, depart from my life now and never return, in the name of Jesus.

6. Any spirit of never do well toward the things of God, depart from my life now and never return, in the name of Jesus.

7. Any spirit of planlessness in my relationship with God, depart now, in the name of Jesus.

8. Any spirit of thoughtlessness in my relationship with God, depart from me now, in the name of Jesus.

9. Forgive me O God for any time in my life that I have presented You with inferior sacrifices, in the name of Jesus.

10. Father Lord, let the same anointing that was upon Abel, which drove him to offer an excellent sacrifice to You, come upon my life now, in the name of Jesus.

11. Lord, that same anointing that was upon Abel that caused him to do well toward You, let it fall upon my life now, in the name of Jesus.

12. Messiah, that same anointing that was upon Abel that caused him to be thorough in his activities toward You, enter into my life now, in the name of Jesus.

13. Father, let that same willingness that was in Abel to expend effort and time and resources and thought toward anything that concerns You, enter into my life now, in the name of Jesus.

14. My God, that same anointing that was upon Abel which caused him to offer You the best of what he had available, let it enter into my life now, in the name of Jesus.

15. Henceforth, O Lord, when it comes to anything to do with You, may I always do the right thing, in the name of Jesus.

16. When it comes to You O Lord, may I not only do the right thing, let me also do the right thing in the correct way, in the name of Jesus.

17. Eternal King, as I offer my sacrifices to You with thoughtfulness, thoroughness, respect and excellence, as it was with Abel, have respect unto my sacrifices and let me find favor in Your sight, in the name of Jesus.

18. Thank You Mighty Father for answering my prayers, in Jesus' mighty name, amen.

CHAPTER 12

FAVOR DUE TO FINDING WISDOM

"For whoso findeth me findeth life, and shall obtain favour of the LORD." — Proverbs 8:35 (KJV)

In Proverbs 8, Wisdom introduces itself elaborately. Here's what it said about its origin:

Proverbs 8:22-27 (KJV) *"The Lord possessed me in the beginning of his way, before his works of old. I was set up from everlasting, from the beginning, or ever the earth was. When there were no depths, I was brought forth; when there were no fountains abounding with water. Before the mountains were settled, before the hills was I brought forth: While as yet he had not made the earth, nor the fields, nor the highest part of the dust of the world. When he prepared the heavens, I was there: when he set a compass upon the face of the depth..."*

Proverbs 8:30-31 (KJV) *"Then I was by him, as one brought up with him: and I was daily his delight, rejoicing always before him; Rejoicing in the habitable part of his earth; and my delights were with the sons of men."*

Wisdom is telling us that before Almighty God ever ventured to create the universe, He first created it and thereafter, used it to create everything including the universe. So, all the valleys, seas, water, mountains, hills, plants, fields, sand, dust, the sky, clouds, outer space, etc. were all created by God using wisdom.

In Proverbs 8:18-21, Wisdom goes further to tell us what human or material benefits it has to offer. They include riches and honor, enduring wealth and prosperity, rich inheritances and full treasuries.

How is Wisdom able to bring these benefits about in people's lives? One way is that it causes certain attributes to manifest in the lives of whomever possesses it. These attributes are stated in Proverbs 8:5-16 and some of them are as follows: an understanding heart, excellent thoughts and words, speaking the truth, hatred for wickedness, words of righteousness, words devoid of perversion, prudence, knowledge, hatred of evil, hatred of pride, hatred of arrogance, hatred of evil behavior, hatred for speaking evil words, sound judgment, making just decisions, excellent leadership, etc. Of course, anyone who has these attributes consistently manifesting in their lives will get the material benefits wisdom has to offer.

The other way that a person can get the benefits of wisdom in their life is stated in our opening scripture, which we will re-state here again for emphasis:

Proverbs 8:35 (KJV) *"For whoso findeth me findeth life, and shall obtain favour of the LORD."*

If you find wisdom, you will obtain the favor of God. As you will see in Part 4 of this book, the favor of God is multifaceted. One dimension of God's favor will get you the material benefits we mentioned earlier. But, recognize that there are many godless people who have material blessings in their lives. So, there is another dimension to God's favor.

Since divine favor means divine recognition, wisdom is also saying that, with it in your life, you will get access to blessings that only God can give you. This includes: direct access to Him, the blessing of His attention, various spiritual blessings, various spiritual gifts, inner joy and peace, divine protection and so on.

So, if finding wisdom is a requirement for obtaining divine favor from the Lord, how then do you get wisdom?

Proverbs 8:17 (KJV) *"I love them that love me; and those that seek me early shall find me."*

Proverbs 2:6 (KJV) *"For the LORD giveth wisdom:* **out of his mouth** *cometh knowledge and understanding."*

Isaiah 11:2 (KJV) *"And the spirit of the LORD shall rest upon him,* **the spirit of wisdom** *and understanding, the spirit of counsel and might, the spirit of knowledge and of the fear of the LORD"*

Deuteronomy 34:9 (KJV) *"And Joshua the son of Nun was full of* **the spirit of wisdom***; for Moses had laid his hands upon him: and the children of Israel hearkened unto him..."*

Getting wisdom requires finding it. And the only place where divine wisdom can be found is from the Lord. You can get divine wisdom surely from the Word of God as stated in scripture. And, as the aforementioned scriptures reveal, there is such a thing as "the spirit of wisdom". In fact, as Moses' ministry was winding down, in order for Israel to have another leader as capable as himself, he had to lay his hands on Joshua, so that he could transfer the spirit of wisdom into his life.

Our prayers in this session will cover—amongst other things—asking the Almighty for the spirit of wisdom, asking for divine favor due to wisdom, asking for the manifestation of the attributes of wisdom, asking for the material benefits of wisdom and asking for the spiritual benefits of divine favor.

PRAYERS

1. Yahweh, I acknowledge the ancient power of wisdom. Make me a beneficiary of this power today, in the name of Jesus.

2. Lord, if You created wisdom before everything else and You are offering it to humans, I am most grateful and I accept Your offering with the whole of my life, in the name of Jesus.

3. Father, Your word says that You used wisdom to manufacture everything in the universe including me. Since I want to live a creative life, I desire this phenomenon in my life, in the name of Jesus.

4. My King and my God, Your word says that only those who seek wisdom shall find it. Here I am seeking it before You today. Have mercy on me and let me find it, in the name of Jesus.

5. Your word says, O Lord, that You give wisdom and out of Your mouth comes knowledge and understanding. Henceforth, I will begin to dig into Your word in order to mine it for wisdom. Have mercy and let me find wisdom from Your word, in the name of Jesus.

6. Word of God, as I open you to read you, henceforth, out of your pages and into my soul shall wisdom be transferred, in the name of Jesus.

7. O God, Your word says that the spirit of wisdom can rest upon a person. Have mercy and let the spirit of wisdom rest

upon me today, in the name of Jesus.

8. In the same manner Moses laid hands on Joshua and he became full of the spirit of wisdom, have mercy on me, Lord. Lay Your hand upon me and let me become full of the spirit of wisdom, in the name of Jesus.

9. That same spirit of wisdom that was upon Joshua, come now and fall upon my life, in the name of Jesus.

10. Lord, Your word says that finding wisdom is obtaining favor from You. By reason of the presence of the spirit of wisdom in my life, Lord, give unto me Your divine favor, in the name of Jesus.

11. I, _____ (your name) possess wisdom and the divine favor of God in my life, in the name of Jesus.

12. Divine favor by reason of divine wisdom is my lot. Begin to manifest in my life now, in the name of Jesus.

13. Now Lord, let all the attributes of wisdom begin to manifest in my life, in the name of Jesus.

14. By reason of wisdom in my life, I claim an understanding heart, in the name of Jesus.

15. By reason of wisdom in my life, I claim excellent thoughts and words, in the name of Jesus.

16. By reason of wisdom in my life, I claim the ability to always speak the truth, in the name of Jesus.

17. By reason of wisdom in my life, I claim hatred for wickedness, in the name of Jesus.

18. By reason of wisdom in my life, I claim the ability to speak words of righteousness, in the name of Jesus.

19. By reason of wisdom in my life, I claim the ability to speak words devoid of perversion, in the name of Jesus.

20. By reason of wisdom in my life, I claim prudence, in the name of Jesus.

21. By reason of wisdom in my life, I claim knowledge, in the name of Jesus.

22. By reason of wisdom in my life, I claim hatred of evil, in the name of Jesus.

23. By reason of wisdom in my life, I claim hatred of pride, in the name of Jesus.

24. By reason of wisdom in my life, I claim hatred of arrogance, in the name of Jesus.

25. By reason of wisdom in my life, I claim hatred of evil behavior, in the name of Jesus.

26. By reason of wisdom in my life, I claim hatred for speaking evil words, in the name of Jesus.

27. By reason of wisdom in my life, I claim sound judgment, in the name of Jesus.

28. By reason of wisdom in my life, I claim the ability to make just decisions, in the name of Jesus.

29. By reason of wisdom in my life, I claim the ability to provide excellent leadership, in the name of Jesus.

30. Everlasting Father, once again, let all these attributes of wisdom begin to manifest in my life, in the name of Jesus.

31. Alpha and Omega, let the presence of Your wisdom and Your divine favor bring me both human and spiritual breakthroughs, in the name of Jesus.

32. Let Your wisdom and Your favor bring me riches and honor, in the name of Jesus.

33. Let Your wisdom and Your favor bring me enduring wealth and prosperity all the days of my life, in the name of Jesus.

34. Let Your wisdom and Your favor give me access to rich inheritances and fill up my treasuries, in the name of Jesus.

35. Let Your divine favor give me direct access to You, O God, in the name of Jesus.

36. Let Your divine favor confer on me the blessing of Your attention, O God, in the name of Jesus.

37. Merciful Father, let Your divine favor usher in various spiritual blessings into my life, in the name of Jesus.

38. King of kings, let Your divine favor deposit Your spiritual gifts into my life, in the name of Jesus.

39. Lord of lords, let Your divine favor bring me inner peace and joy, in the name of Jesus.

40. Almighty God, let Your divine favor enable Your divine protection in my life, in the name of Jesus.

41. Let Your divine favor cause me to complete my race on earth with victory, in the name of Jesus.

42. Thank You Father for the phenomenon of wisdom and for making me a beneficiary, in the name of Jesus.

43. Thank You Lord for the phenomenon of divine favor and for making me a beneficiary, in the name of Jesus.

44. Thank You Mighty God for answering my prayers, in Jesus' mighty name, amen.

CHAPTER 13

FAVOR DUE TO TRUTH & FAITHFULNESS

"Let not mercy and truth forsake thee: bind them about thy neck; write them upon the table of thine heart: So shalt thou find favour and good understanding in the sight of God and man."
— Proverbs 3:3-4 (KJV)

Our penultimate examination of the requirements of divine favor lands us on a requirement that has two interpretations, both of which if fulfilled, will cause you to find favor in the sight of God as well as humans. These interpretations of our opening scripture are as follows:

1. Preventing separation from the Mercy and the Truth of God

In our first interpretation, our opening scripture is essentially saying that favor is the reward of those who possess the mercy and truth of the Almighty.

Romans 9:15 (KJV) *"I will have mercy on whom I will have mercy, and I will have compassion on whom I will have compassion."*

2 Timothy 4:3-4 (KJV) *"For the time will come when they will not endure sound doctrine; but after their own lusts shall they heap to themselves teachers, having itching ears; And they shall turn away their ears from the truth, and shall be turned unto fables."*

When you are a beneficiary of the mercy and compassion of God, it simply means that for both the things you ask for and those you do not ask for, He will be willing to do for you. Anyone fortunate enough to be in this situation, of course, is a candidate of favor with God and people.

Also, the truth means sound doctrine. And this sound doctrine comes from reading or listening to the word of God. If God spent time speaking and inspiring saints of old to write down His words, and you, in this mostly ungodly generation, decide to spend your time to read that word or listen to it, God will favor you and cause you to have favor before people as well. If in this generation, where people appoint unto themselves teachers who—through the use of fables and lies—cause them to ultimately forsake the truth, you decide to thirst for sound doctrine, God will reward you with favor before Him and other people.

Therefore, securing the mercy and truth of God must be one of your greatest desires. And, if you have already tasted of God's mercy before and you want more of it AND if you are a lover of sound doctrine and you want to keep reaping divine favor, never do anything that will cause God to make His mercy forsake you. And never let your desire for sound doctrine perish.

. . .

2. Fortitude to continue being merciful and faithful.

The second interpretation puts the ball firmly in your court. In this case, the word "truth" actually means "faithfulness"; as in when someone says *"Always be true to yourself"* or *"You are the true son of your father"*. So, we can say truth here means faithfulness or fidelity or dependability or trustworthiness.

If you rephrase our opening verse, it would now read something like "Let not mercy and truth or faithfulness or dependability or trustworthiness forsake thee".

In the first interpretation, it was mainly God's show. Here, it's your show somewhat. Here, it is your responsibility to be merciful to other people and to be faithful unto both God and other people.

Matthew 5:7 (KJV) *"Blessed are the merciful: for they shall obtain mercy."*

Numbers 30:2 (KJV) *"If a man vow a vow unto the LORD, or swear an oath to bind his soul with a bond; he shall not break his word, he shall do according to all that proceedeth out of his mouth."*

Matthew 25:21 (KJV) *"His lord said unto him, Well done, thou good and faithful servant: thou hast been faithful over a few things, I will make thee ruler over many things: enter thou into the joy of thy lord."*

If you show people mercy and you do not let that attribute leave you all the days of your life, the Lord will in turn grant you favor before Himself and other people. Also, if you consistently make promises to God and to others and you consistently keep them, the Lord will in turn give you favor before Himself and other people.

. . .

PRAYERS

1. Holy One of Israel, let me enjoy Your favor all the days of my life, in the name of Jesus.

2. King of kings, all the days of my life, let me enjoy favor before people who will move my life forward, in the name of Jesus.

3. Lord, regardless of what path I am required to take, I am prepared to do whatever I need to in order to become and remain a candidate of Your favor. Help me win, in the name of Jesus.

4. My God, Your word reveals that if I do not let Your mercy forsake me, You will give me favor before Yourself and before people. Let this be my portion in life, in the name of Jesus.

5. Everlasting Father, Your word says that You give mercy and compassion to whomever You desire. I declare that my life is available. Let Your mercy locate me and enter into my life, in the name of Jesus.

6. Henceforth, O God, let Your mercy be bound around my neck and never come off, in the name of Jesus.

7. Henceforth, O Lord, let Your mercy be written upon the table of my heart, in the name of Jesus.

8. Almighty God, I declare that I am a lover of Your sound doctrine. Let every blessing attached to addiction to and practice of sound doctrine, come into my life now, in the name of Jesus.

9. Henceforth, O God, as I read or listen to Your truth, let it be bound around my neck so that I can always remember to do it, in the name of Jesus.

10. My God, let Your word that I read and Your sound doctrine that I listen to be written upon the table of my heart so I can never forget to live them out, in the name of Jesus.

11. I reject the lust of deceitful teachers. I refuse to be deceived, in the name of Jesus.

12. I reject the fables of false teachers. My ears will never be turned away from the truth, in the name of Jesus.

13. O Lord, may I never do anything that will cause Your mercy to forsake me, in the name of Jesus.

14. Be merciful unto me, Father. May I never do anything that will cause the truth to depart from my life, in the name of Jesus.

15. Now Lord, by reason of Your mercy and truth in my life, let me find favor and good understanding in Your sight and in the sight of people, in the name of Jesus.

16. O Lord, Your word says that the blessing of the merciful is that they will obtain mercy. May this be my portion, in the name of Jesus.

17. Forgive me, O lord, if I have not been a merciful person up till this point in my life. From today, I turn a new leaf. I ask for the grace to become and remain merciful unto others, in the name of Jesus.

18. Henceforth, Father, let the mind be in me that if someone is in need of cash or kind or knowledge and I have the cash or kind or knowledge they need in abundance, I shall give it to them, in the name of Jesus.

19. Jehovah, transform me. Make me into a person of genuine compassion with only You to impress, in the name of Jesus.

20. Now Lord, I ask, make me into a person of truth, in the name of Jesus.

21. Make me into a person of faithfulness, in the name of Jesus.

22. Make me into a dependable person, in the name of Jesus.

23. Make me into a trustworthy person, in the name of Jesus.

24. Lord, let it be that whenever I say either to You or to a fellow human being that I will do something, I will do that thing, in the name of Jesus.

25. Father, I shall not be a disappointment. Let it be that whatever I cannot do, I will always say that I cannot do, in the name of Jesus.

26. My God, by reason of my acts of mercy unto my fellow human beings, let me find favor before You and before people, in the name of Jesus.

27. Rock of Ages, by reason of my truthfulness and my trustworthiness, give me favor before You and before people, in the name of Jesus.

28. Let me reap the fruit of my obedience to Your word, in the name of Jesus.

29. Let me become a shining example of what it means to possess divine favor in this generation, in the name of Jesus.

30. Thank You Heavenly Father for answering my prayers, in Jesus' mighty name, amen.

CHAPTER 14
FAVOR DUE TO LOWLINESS

"Surely he (God) scorneth the scorners: but he giveth grace unto the lowly." — Proverbs 3:33-35 (KJV)

For reasons best known to Him, God loves lowly people. In addition to our opening scripture, here are some scriptures that effectively illustrate this:

Psalm 138:6 (KJV) *"Though the LORD be high, **yet hath he respect unto the lowly**: but the proud he knoweth afar off."*

Job 5:8-11 (KJV) *"I would seek unto God, and unto God would I commit my cause: Which doeth great things and unsearchable; marvellous things without number: Who giveth rain upon the earth, and sendeth waters upon the fields: **To set up on high those that be low**..."*

Matthew 11:29 (KJV) *"Take my yoke upon you, and learn of me; for I am meek and **lowly in heart**: and ye shall find rest unto your souls."*

Not only does God prefer the lowly, when He Himself came into this world as Jesus Christ, the last scripture we just read says that He chose to be "lowly in heart".

What does it mean to be lowly in heart? A person who is lowly in heart, in this session's context, is one who is full of humility regardless of their actual level or status in life. He or she has made the decision, of their own volition, to be modest no matter what.

So, how do you practice lowliness of heart? Since Jesus Christ introduced the concept of lowliness of heart, He only can provide a guide for practicing it, and He does. Let's examine how He does this from scripture:

Luke 14:1 (KJV) *"And it came to pass, as he (Jesus) went into the house of one of the chief Pharisees to eat bread on the sabbath day, that they watched him..."*

Luke 14:7-9 (KJV) *"...And he put forth a parable to those which were bidden, when he marked how they chose out the chief rooms; saying unto them. When thou art bidden of any man to a wedding, sit not down in the highest room; lest a more honourable man than thou be bidden of him; And he that bade thee and him come and say to thee, Give this man place; and thou begin with shame to take the lowest room."*

Luke 14:10-11 (KJV) *"But when thou art bidden, go and sit down in the lowest room; that when he that bade thee cometh, he may say unto thee, Friend, go up higher: then shalt thou have worship in the presence of them that sit at meat with thee. For whosoever exalteth himself shall be abased; and he that humbleth himself shall be exalted."*

What beautiful words! And what powerful insight into how Almighty God runs the universe.

Jesus had been invited to an event at the house of a chief phar-
isee and when He got there, He noticed how other invited
people were scampering to take the most important seats. He
then used what He witnessed to explain how lowliness of heart
works. The event organizer knows who he has invited and he
has already designated seats for everyone. Since you—the
guest—do not know what your designated seat is or if you
even have a designated seat, when you arrive, sit on the lowest
seat there.

Let's assume a book author is organizing an event such as a
book launch. For this specific event, the most important
people to him or her are his family members, his editor, his
publisher, his graphic designer, his marketer, his distributor, his
devoted readers, his staff and other people directly involved in
his field. So, if the publisher or distributor or any of these
aforementioned people arrives at the event and sits at the very
back, it doesn't matter. When the event starts, the author "will
definitely" bring the publisher or the distributor to the high
table meant for the dignitaries. And as this person walks
towards the high table, it would usually be to rounds of
applause. What an honor!

However, if someone else not central to the author's efforts to
release the book arrives and sits at the high table, even if he or
she was invited, because the seats have been designated for the
most important people, the author will have no choice but to
ask that person to leave the high table. What a shameful
predicament! And, because the event has already started, such
a person would only find the worst seat, if any at all.

God knows the hearts of all mankind. He knows who is important to Him and who is not. We are all in the event of life. We
have all been invited to the part of humanity in this world.

Believers, who are lowly in heart, are the most important people to God. Sitting on the high table of life means getting access to His blessings, good health, long life, spiritual depth, spiritual gifts and the assurance of eternity in heaven. The ticket that will move anyone from the general area to the high table of life is the ticket of lowliness stamped with, as our opening scripture says, the grace or the divine favor of God.

PRAYERS

1. Father, I have learned today another way that You have established the universe to work. I am here to apply myself and benefit from it. Help me, in the name of Jesus.

2. Adonai, give me the heart to turn back if it is obvious to me that I am heading in the wrong direction, in the name of Jesus.

3. I want to fulfill my destiny on earth. Therefore, today, I depart from the path of arrogance and step into the way of humility, in the name of Jesus.

4. Every spirit of pride in my life, depart from me now and never return, in the name of Jesus.

5. Every arrow of self-exaltation fired against my destiny in order to bring me shame, depart from my life now, in the name of Jesus.

6. I repent of the sins of pride and self-exaltation. Have mercy, Lord, and forgive me, in the name of Jesus.

7. My God, if Jesus was lowly in heart while He was here, I desire to be as well. Help me, in the name of Jesus.

8. My Savior was lowly, I too will be lowly, in the name of Jesus.

9. Lord, let my heart, henceforth, be filled with humility, in the name of Jesus.

10. Alpha, let my mouth speak words soaked in humility, in the name of Jesus.

11. Omega, infuse in me the grace to act or behave humbly in my conduct with You and with people, in the name of Jesus.

12. Henceforth, even though I live a life of high ambition and high achievement, in my dealings with You and other people, I will live a life of modest speech and modest behavior, in the name of Jesus.

13. In the same manner Jesus had the highest ambition of saving mankind from perishing and yet was lowly in heart, I too shall fulfill my ambitions while being lowly in heart, in speech and in conduct, in the name of Jesus.

14. By reason of divine lowliness in my heart, I will never be put to shame, in the name of Jesus.

15. By reason of divine lowliness in my life, I will never be embarrassed or disgraced, in the name of Jesus.

16. By reason of divine lowliness in my life, the grace and divine favor of Almighty God shall locate me, in the name of Jesus.

17. By reason of divine lowliness in my life, divine favor shall summon me from the general area to the high table of life, in the name of Jesus.

18. Oh Lord, stamp my ticket of lowliness with Your divine favor so I can be summoned to the high table of life, in the name of Jesus.

19. Divine favor by reason of divine lowliness shall cause me to enjoy the *material blessings of God* on the high table of life, in the name of Jesus.

20. Divine favor by reason of divine lowliness shall cause me to enjoy **good health** on the high table of life, in the name of Jesus.

21. Divine favor by reason of divine lowliness shall cause me to enjoy **long life** on the high table of life, in the name of Jesus.

22. Divine favor by reason of divine lowliness shall cause me to enjoy **spiritual depth** on the high table of life, in the name of Jesus.

23. Divine favor by reason of divine lowliness shall cause me to enjoy **spiritual gifts** on the high table of life, in the name of Jesus.

24. Divine favor by reason of divine lowliness shall cause me to receive **the assurance of eternal life**, in the name of Jesus.

25. Thank You Lord for answering my prayers, in Jesus' mighty name, amen.

PART IV

PRAYERS FOR DIVERSE MANIFESTATIONS OF DIVINE FAVOR IN YOUR LIFE

This part shows the diverse manifestations of divine favor in the lives of people and prayers to get the manifestations replicated in your life.

CHAPTER 15
FAVOR FOR SALVATION

"Remember me, O LORD, with the favour that thou bearest unto thy people: O visit me with thy salvation"
— Psalm 106:4 (KJV)

PURPOSE

This prayer session is:

- For repenting from sin
- For the salvation of your soul
- For escape from hellfire
- For making the rapture
- For eternal security in heaven

PRAYERS

1. Holy One of Israel, it is only because you love with an ever-lasting love that I can stand before You today to make these prayers. To You be all the glory and praise, in the name of Jesus.

2. Lord, I know that hell is a place of torment. I do not want to go there. Therefore, I ask: Let me find grace in Your eyes and be saved from hell, in the name of Jesus.

3. Adonai, I know that right now, there are people suffering eternal punishment in the fires of hell. Make Your face shine upon me and save me from this kind of damnation, in the name of Jesus.

4. Jehovah Tsidkenu, I did not come into this world only to end up in eternal suffering. Have mercy on me and save me, in the name of Jesus.

5. My Father and my God, once again I call out to You: do not let me enter into the everlasting pit filled with lost souls who are being tormented in heat and by worms that never die. Have regard for my prayers today and save me, in the name of Jesus.

6. Lord, I believe in You and in Your son, Jesus Christ. I believe that He sacrificed himself so that anyone can be saved. I choose to be saved. Redeem me today, redeem me now, in the name of Jesus.

7. Messiah, I know that my life is not free of faults. Be gracious unto me and forgive me these faults, in the name of Jesus.

8. O Righteous Father, without a doubt, I make moral mistakes. Be gracious unto me and forgive me these mistakes, in the name of Jesus.

9. Conqueror of sin, be gracious unto me and forgive me for all my negative or evil thoughts, in the name of Jesus.

10. Have mercy O Lord and deliver me from all the negative traits and behaviors in my life, in the name of Jesus.

11. O God, sometimes my spiritual ignorance pushes me to rationalize my sins. Let me obtain favor from You. Deliver me from my ignorance, in the name of Jesus.

12. Father, break me free powerfully from the power of sin, in the name of Jesus.

13. King of kings, make me the object of Your goodwill and sanctify me, in the name of Jesus.

14. Lord of lords, cause me to be free from sin, in the name of Jesus.

15. Eternal King, have compassion on me and certify me holy, in the name of Jesus.

16. My God, make me acceptable unto You, in the name of Jesus.

17. O Lord, I pray: By reason of Your redemptive work in my life, save me from eternal harm, in the name of Jesus.

18. O Lord, save me from eternal ruin, in the name of Jesus.

19. O Lord, rescue me from eternal loss, in the name of Jesus.

20. O Lord, rescue me from eternal destruction, in the name of Jesus.

21. My God, do not let me be separated from You or lost from You without hope. Anchor my destiny to Your grace, in the name of Jesus.

22. By reason of Your eternal grace upon my life, Righteous Father, I declare that I will never be a resident of hell, in the name of Jesus.

23. There will never come a time that I will close my eyes here on earth only to find myself in darkness and inside the fires of hell, in the name of Jesus.

24. By reason of your redemptive work, O Lord, I will never find myself in the midst of the eternally damned and eternally lost, in the name of Jesus.

25. Now Lord, I ask: Make Your face shine upon me and let my name be written in heaven, in the name of Jesus.

26. Father, if I have found grace in Your sight, let my name be written in the Book of Life permanently, in the name of Jesus.

27. Holy Father, be favorable unto me and make me a candidate of eternal life in heaven, in the name of Jesus.

28. I declare that, because I have obtained favor from You, O Lord, if my eyes close here on this earth, they shall open in the City of God and nowhere else, in the name of Jesus.

29. I declare that, because the divine favor of God has been activated in my life, whenever the trumpet sounds and I am still alive, I shall hear it and be caught up in the clouds with my Lord and Savior and with millions of saints, with whom I shall enter into heaven, in the name of Jesus.

30. Thank You Great and Mighty God for Your favor upon my life and for answering my prayers, in Jesus' mighty name, amen.

CHAPTER 16

FAVOR FOR DIVINE RESCUE

"Turn us again, O God, and cause thy face to shine; and we shall be saved." — Psalm 80:3 (KJV)

PURPOSE

This prayer session is:

- For divine rescue from the diverse difficulties of life
- For a problem-free life
- For obtaining the freedom to make progress in life
- For becoming free to pursue and fulfill destiny

PRAYERS

1. O God, activate Your divine favor in my life, in the name of Jesus.

2. Father, let Your favor repel any arrow of difficulty shot at my life, in the name of Jesus.

3. Any arrow of problems fired against me, I command you: return to sender, in the name of Jesus.

4. I am a candidate of the kindness of God. Therefore, no spirit and no human can hassle me, in the name of Jesus.

5. I am a beneficiary of divine favor, therefore, afflictions shall have no place in my life, in the name of Jesus.

6. Lord God Almighty, I intreat Your favor with my whole heart. Let every burden of worry upon my heart be lifted completely, in the name of Jesus.

7. Distress shall not be my portion, in the name of Jesus.

8. O Lord, my High Tower, shield me against any nightmare attacks, in the name of Jesus.

9. Because I enjoy the favor of the Lord, my nightlife and my dream life will never become a battleground, in the name of Jesus.

10. Because I enjoy the favor of the Lord, I shall sleep and wake in peace, in the name of Jesus.

11. Make Your face shine upon me, O Lord, and deliver me from any danger assigned against me, in the name of Jesus.

12. Make Your face shine upon me, my Father, and stop me from making any mistake that will bring me loss, in the name of Jesus.

13. Heavenly Father, shield me from the spirit of confusion that has befallen so many, in the name of Jesus.

14. I reject any spirit of confusion of identity, confusion about self, in the name of Jesus.

15. By the grace and mercy of God, misfortune shall not be my portion, in the name of Jesus.

16. My going out and coming in are blessed of the Lord, in the name of Jesus.

17. O Lord, turn Your face toward me and shield me from any sort of struggle, in the name of Jesus.

18. I refuse to struggle with the knowledge of who I am in Christ, in the name of Jesus.

19. I refuse to struggle professionally, in the name of Jesus.

20. I refuse to struggle emotionally, in the name of Jesus.

21. I will not struggle financially, in the name of Jesus.

22. Father, in Your mercy, do not leave me to face any turmoil. Shield me from all forms of turmoil, in the name of Jesus.

23. Let me benefit from Your kindness O Lord by resolving any misunderstanding I have with anyone and by preventing any new misunderstanding from arising between me and anyone, in the name of Jesus.

24. Let me benefit from Your mercy O Lord by taking away strife from my environment, in the name of Jesus.

25. Any spirit of strife assigned against me, Listen to me: I am not Your candidate. Depart from my life and never return, in the name of Jesus.

26. Because I am favored of the Lord, I shall never be the target of any campaign of embarrassment, in the name of Jesus.

27. Anyone planning to embarrass me for any reason, be exposed and face divine judgment, in the name of Jesus.

28. Divine Favor of the Most High God, arise for my sake and clear off all hindrances on my path of progress, in the name of Jesus.

29. Divine Favor of the Almighty, show up and deliver me from all my fears, in the name of Jesus.

30. O Lord, be favorable unto me and deliver me from any form of hardship, in the name of Jesus.

31. Deliver me from hardships of the body, in the name of Jesus.

32. Deliver me from hardships related to my work, in the name of Jesus.

33. Deliver me from hardships of the pocket, in the name of Jesus.

34. Save me, O Lord, in Your mercy, and rescue me from all nuisances, in the name of Jesus.

35. Separate me from all nuisance situations, in the name of Jesus.

36. Father, put a wall of delineation between me and nuisance people, in the name of Jesus.

37. I refuse to be dragged down by any son or daughter of satan, in the name of Jesus.

38. I will never be dragged back into sin by sons and daughters of the devil, in the name of Jesus.

39. Have compassion on me, O God, and let any vexation of my spirit be halted permanently, in the name of Jesus.

40. Any strange spirit attempting to unleash vexation of spirit and even of body and soul upon me, my life is not your candidate. Depart from me and never return, in the name of Jesus.

41. Lord, be generous unto me, deliver me from the spirit of panic, in the name of Jesus.

42. Lord, let it be that no matter the situation, I shall stand strong, in the name of Jesus.

43. Lord, be generous unto me and rescue me from the spirit of controversy, in the name of Jesus.

44. From today, I shall no longer be embroiled in any controversy again, in the name of Jesus.

45. Lord, show me Your favor and rescue me from the hands of the spirit of wastage, in the name of Jesus.

46. Any problem designed to waste my time, I am not your candidate. Return to sender, in the name of Jesus.

47. Any problem designed to waste my attention, return to sender, in the name of Jesus.

48. Any problem designed to waste my resources, return to sender, in the name of Jesus.

49. Switch on Your favor in my life, O God, and shield me from all forms of calamities, in the name of Jesus.

50. The calamity that easily besets others will never ever befall me, in the name of Jesus.

51. Give Your grace to me, O Lord and do not let other people hear bad news from me or about me, in the name of Jesus.

52. Be gracious, O God, and do not let me hear bad news from or concerning my loved ones, in the name of Jesus.

53. Catastrophe shall never be my portion, in the name of Jesus.

54. I shall live until a good old age and die in peace. No catastrophe shall end my life, in the name of Jesus.

55. Even if dire times envelope my city or my country, because I am divinely favored, I shall experience goodly times always, in the name of Jesus.

56. Even if misery fills the world, I shall rise above it all because I am favored of the Lord, in the name of Jesus.

57. El Shaddai, let me increase in favor with You until such an extent that travails shall be a thing of the past in my life, in the name of Jesus.

58. Lord, let me increase in favor with You to such an extent that desperation shall become a thing of the past in my life, in the name of Jesus.

59. I shall not become the victim of any kind of disturbance, in the name of Jesus.

60. I shall not become the victim of any kind of chaos, in the name of Jesus.

61. No man or woman shall be able to punish me, because I have found favor in the eyes of the Lord, in the name of Jesus.

62. Because I have found favor in the eyes of the Lord, grief will not be my portion, in the name of Jesus.

63. The favor of the Lord upon my life shields me from all forms of harassment, in the name of Jesus.

64. The favor of the Lord shields me from any kind of molestation, in the name of Jesus.

65. Since the Lord knows me by name, I am exempted from diseases, in the name of Jesus.

66. Since the Lord knows me by name, all adversaries, clear out of my path, in the name of Jesus.

67. Since the Lord knows me by name, all stumbling blocks, clear out of my way, in the name of Jesus.

68. The voice of favor in my life shall speak louder than the voice of envy against me, in the name of Jesus.

69. The voice of favor in my life shall drown out the voice of hatred against me, in the name of Jesus.

70. The voice of favor in my life shall silence any false accusation fashioned against me, in the name of Jesus.

71. Because I have found favor in the eyes of the Lord, I shall never be in jeopardy, in the name of Jesus.

72. Favor will always be with me to keep me safe from all perils, in the name of Jesus.

73. I am a candidate of God's kindness, therefore, I can never be in a tight spot, in the name of Jesus.

74. I am a beneficiary of God's mercy, therefore, I can never be boxed into a tight corner, in the name of Jesus.

75. No threat of the enemy shall ever materialize against me, in the name of Jesus.

76. I shall never be a victim, neither shall I ever be brought down by any slippery slope, in the name of Jesus.

77. The trap of the enemy shall never catch me, in the name of Jesus.

78. Lord, since You have regard for my prayers, I know that I shall never enter into the deathtrap of the enemy, in the name of Jesus.

79. The favor of the Lord gives me freedom to be who I should be without fear of what the enemy shall do to me, and it gives me the allowance I need to fulfill my destiny, in the name of Jesus.

80. Thank You Father God for Your favor in answering my prayers, in Jesus' mighty name, amen.

CHAPTER 17

FAVOR FOR PRESERVATION OF SPIRIT

"Thou hast granted me life and favour, and thy visitation hath preserved my spirit." — Job 10:12 (KJV)

PURPOSE

This prayer session is:

- For protection against untimely death
- For the preservation of your life
- For good health
- For maximum vitality

PRAYERS

1. O great and awesome God, You hold life and death in Your hands. Take away death from me and give me life, in the name of Jesus.

2. If I have found favor before You, O Lord, I ask that You take action today to save my life, in the name of Jesus.

3. Since You have granted me Your favor, O Lord, take action to protect my life, in the name of Jesus.

4. I do not want to die an untimely death. Therefore Lord, I ask: visit me in order to preserve my spirit, in the name of Jesus.

5. Let Your visitation save me from the spirit of death, in the name of Jesus.

6. Let Your visitation preserve my body and keep it from the hand of the destroyer, in the name of Jesus.

7. Let Your visitation preserve my soul, in the name of Jesus.

8. Let Your visitation preserve my spirit and keep it from the gates of death and hell, in the name of Jesus.

9. I have obtained the favor of the Lord, therefore, I shall not die an untimely death, in the name of Jesus.

10. I have obtained the favor of the Lord, therefore, I shall not be killed, in the name of Jesus.

11. I have obtained the favor of the Lord, therefore, I shall not expire before my time, in the name of Jesus.

12. I have obtained the favor of the Lord, therefore, my loved ones will not lose me before my time, in the name of Jesus.

13. I have obtained the favor of the Lord, therefore, I shall not be cut down, in the name of Jesus.

14. I have obtained the favor of the Lord, therefore, I shall never ever fall to suicide, in the name of Jesus.

15. I have obtained the favor of the Lord, therefore, no man or woman can waste me, in the name of Jesus.

16. I have obtained the favor of the Lord, therefore, I shall not be numbered amongst the departed before my time, in the name of Jesus.

17. The goodwill of the Lord upon my life mandates that whenever I go to sleep, I shall arise. I shall not die in my sleep before my time, in the name of Jesus.

18. Until I am advanced in years, I shall not fall silent suddenly, in the name of Jesus.

19. Until I am advanced in age, I shall not be discovered unresponsive, in the name of Jesus.

20. Until I am advanced in years, whenever I am woken up, I shall wake up and resume life, in the name of Jesus.

21. O God, extend Your favor and Your support to me and let me be alert and active all the days of my life, in the name of Jesus.

22. O God, extend Your favor and Your kindness to me and let me be whole all the days of my life, in the name of Jesus.

23. Father, extend Your favor and Your benevolence to me and let me bask in the land of the living until a good old age, in the name of Jesus.

24. Be gracious unto me, O Lord and keep me safe from injury, in the name of Jesus.

25. If I have found favor in Your eyes, O Lord, maintain my life in good health and keep me intact until a good old age, in the name of Jesus.

26. I shall remain vitalized all the days of my life, in the name of Jesus.

27. I shall remain animated all the days of my life, in the name of Jesus.

28. The favor of the Lord confers upon me the vigor of the Lord, in the name of Jesus.

29. The favor of the Lord confers upon me the liveliness of the Lord, in the name of Jesus.

30. I have held on to the helping hand of the Lord, therefore, I have received divine health in my blood, in the name of Jesus.

31. The helping hand of the Lord is upon my head, therefore, my spirit is in service, in the name of Jesus.

32. The helping hand of the Lord is upon my head, therefore, my spirit is in working order, in the name of Jesus.

33. Have compassion on me Lord and maintain me, in the name of Jesus.

34. Have compassion upon me Lord and sustain me, in the name of Jesus.

35. Show me Your kindness, Father, and prolong my life, in the name of Jesus.

36. Give me Your divine backing, Messiah, and keep me going in life, in the name of Jesus.

37. Lord, as I increase in Your favor, let my contract with life be extended, in the name of Jesus.

38. I have God's divine backing, I have the strength of the Lord, in the name of Jesus.

39. Merciful God, my life is in Your hands. Watch over me, in the name of Jesus.

40. Thank You for showing me Your kindness and for answering my prayers, in Jesus' mighty name, amen.

CHAPTER 18

FAVOR FOR DELIVERANCE
FROM CAPTIVITY

"To the chief Musician, A Psalm for the sons of Korah.
LORD, thou hast been favourable unto thy land: thou
hast brought back the captivity of Jacob."
— Psalm 85:1 (KJV)

PURPOSE

This prayer session is:

- For deliverance from captivity
- For total restoration
- For return to a prosperous state

PRAYERS

1. Holy and true God, I want my life to return to a problem-free state. Since only You can do this, let me find favor with You as I make my prayers now, in the name of Jesus.

2. Lord, Your word says that You changed the sad condition of the children of Israel. Come and change any sad situation in my life today, in the name of Jesus.

3. Your word says that You delivered the Israelites from captivity. Come and deliver me from captivity today, in the name of Jesus.

4. Lord, You saved Your children from affliction, come and save me from affliction today, in the name of Jesus.

5. Father, You restored the Israelites back to a desirable state. Let this also be my portion today, in the name of Jesus.

6. O Lord God Almighty, Your word says that You restored the fortunes of Jacob. Restore my own fortunes today, in the name of Jesus.

7. Eternal King, bring me into Your fellowship of divine favor and let any spiritual chain of captivity on my hands be broken completely, in the name of Jesus.

8. Turn Your face to me O Lord and let any confinement against me be shattered to pieces in the name of Jesus.

9. As no one can confine the wind, may I not be confined by any power or any person, in the name of Jesus.

10. God of Justice, stretch Your hand of favor toward me and let every restraint designed to hold me down be broken permanently, in the name of Jesus.

11. Make Your face shine upon me O Lord, and let me break away from any limitation set against me, in the name of Jesus.

12. Elohim, let me benefit from Your divine fondness fo me today. Forcefully eject me from any yoke of enslavement, in the name of Jesus.

13. Benevolent God, deliver me from servitude today, in the name of Jesus.

14. Light of the world, deliver me from any form of spiritual darkness, in the name of Jesus.

15. Alpha, deliver me from any form of subjugation today, in the name of Jesus.

16. Henceforth, no more subjugation in my life, in the name of Jesus.

17. By reason of the favor of God upon my life, henceforth, no more suppression of my destiny, in the name of Jesus.

18. My destiny must shine and must be fulfilled, in the name of Jesus.

19. Favor of God, break me free from any form of repression, in the name of Jesus.

20. May I never be repressed again. No more inhibiting of my glory, in the name of Jesus.

21. Set me free completely, O Lord, in the name of Jesus.

22. Liberate me completely, O Lord, in the name of Jesus.

23. Unchain me completely, O Lord, in the name of Jesus.

24. Unbind me completely, O Lord, in the name of Jesus.

25. Father, loose me from all bondages so that I can resume my journey of destiny, in the name of Jesus.

26. Now Lord, I ask; if I have found favor in Your eyes, let my destiny be rebuilt in a way that will honor You, in the name of Jesus.

27. Enable Your favor in my life, Messiah, and let my life be reconstructed in a way that pleases You, in the name of Jesus.

28. Make Your face shine upon me and let my glory be rejuvenated, in the name of Jesus.

29. Turn Your face toward me O Lord and let my life be completely regenerated, in the name of Jesus.

30. Touch me Lord with Your hand of favor and revitalize my life, in the name of Jesus.

31. Great Architect, feel free to redesign and reassemble my life so I can fulfill destiny, in the name of Jesus.

32. Assist me O Lord to restore my life to full power and strength, in the name of Jesus.

33. Regard me again, O Lord, and renovate my glory to Your taste, in the name of Jesus.

34. Father, let that which has been stolen from my destiny be returned multiple-fold, in the name of Jesus.

35. Jehovah, my _____ (whatever has been stolen from you) has been stolen. If I have found favor in Your eyes, have mercy and let it be returned to me, in the name of Jesus.

36. The favor of the Lord is upon me, therefore, no more captivity, in the name of Jesus.

37. The favor of the Lord is upon me, therefore, I am restored, in the name of Jesus.

38. The favor of the Lord is upon me, therefore, I am made whole, in the name of Jesus.

39. God's favor is upon me, therefore, I am complete, in the name of Jesus.

40. Thank You O God for Your graciousness in answering my prayers, in Jesus' mighty name, amen.

CHAPTER 19

FAVOR FOR DIVINE VISITATION THAT ENDS DELAY

"And said, My Lord, if now I have found favour in thy sight, pass not away, I pray thee, from thy servant"
— Genesis 18:3 (KJV)

PURPOSE

This prayer session is:

- For divine visitation
- As it was for Abraham and Sarah, for ending delay.
- For divine favor that fulfills long-held desires

NOTE: Our opening scripture in this chapter refers to the moment when angels came to visit Abraham for a number of reasons including to announce the imminent arrival of their long-awaited child. In other words, they came to announce the end to the delay Abraham and Sarah had been experiencing. This chapter includes prayers for ending delay after the pattern of this couple. However, you only know what your long-held desire is. Therefore, wherever you see gaps in the prayers, feel free to insert your desire therein. Blessings.

PRAYERS

1. Prayer answering God, I have come before You today to inform You of my long-held desire. I want You to cause it to manifest at last. Favor me and answer my prayers, in the name of Jesus.

2. O Mighty God, my long-held desire is _____ (mention your long-held desire). Favor me and answer all my prayers concerning it today, in the name of Jesus.

3. Any evil power causing the manifestation of _____ (long-held desire) to happen later rather than sooner, be nullified, in the name of Jesus.

4. Lord, let me see Your face with joy. Cause my wait concerning _____ (long-held desire) to come to an end, in the name of Jesus.

5. Father, _____ (long-held desire) should have manifested a long time ago in my life, but this has not happened. Be merciful unto me and provoke its manifestation, in the name of Jesus.

6. My Father in heaven, the arrival of _____ (long-held desire) is now late. Have compassion on me and let its arrival be sped up, in the name of Jesus.

7. O my Father, if there is any evil power slowing down the materialization of _____ (long-held desire) in my life, let that power be arrested and destroyed, in the name of Jesus.

8. If there be any evil power hindering the appearance of _____ (long-held desire), I bind you and I cast you out of my life, in the name of Jesus.

9. Any foul spirit that may be blocking the emergence of _____ (long-held desire) in my life, be arrested and be banished from my vicinity, in the name of Jesus.

10. I command any evil thing putting off the arrival of _____ (long-held desire) in my life to die, in the name of Jesus.

11. Any evil entity causing the manifestation of _____ (long-held desire) in my life to be deferred, I rebuke you. Your time is up. Get out of my life and never return, in the name of Jesus.

12. Any evil location where the embodiment of my _____ (long-held desire) is being detained, receive the arrows of fire of the Most High and be destroyed, in the name of Jesus.

13. _____ (long-held desire) be released and locate me, in the name of Jesus.

14. You _____ (long-held desire), let whatever evil that is causing you to crawl to me instead of running to me, die, in the name of Jesus.

15. My Shepherd, stretch unto me Your hand of blessing to provoke the manifestation of _____ (long-held desire) in my life, in the name of Jesus.

16. Lord, let me find grace in Your eyes. Visit me in Your power and might and let every pause in the manifestation of _____ (long-held desire) be removed, in the name of Jesus.

17. Divine Favor of God, let any interlude in the manifestation of _____ (long-held desire) in my life be removed, in the name of Jesus.

18. Divine Favor of God, let any command that has halted the arrival of _____ (long-held desire) in my life be revoked, in the name of Jesus.

19. Let any gap between me and _____ (long-held desire) be closed now, in the name of Jesus.

20. Let any holdup blocking _____ (long-held desire) from reaching me be eased or scattered, in the name of Jesus.

21. Let any obstruction blocking the path of _____ (long-held desire) to me smashed to pieces, in the name of Jesus.

22. Any dark power that has placed my _____ (long-held desire) under arrest, be arrested, release my blessing and catch fire, in the name of Jesus.

23. Any evil command that has been issued for the arrival of my _____ (long-held desire) to be carried over indefinitely, be revoked now, in the name of Jesus.

24. Lord, visit me and extend Your hand of generosity to me and help me, in the name of Jesus.

25. Father, favor me and give my requests Your divine backing, in the name of Jesus.

26. Father, visit me and let the manifestation of _____ (long-held desire) in my life be accelerated, in the name of Jesus.

27. O God, visit me and let the arrival of _____ (long-held desire) in my life be hastened, in the name of Jesus.

28. O Lord, visit me and expedite the onset of _____ (long-held desire) in my life, in the name of Jesus.

29. Divine Favor of God, quicken the time it will take for _____ (long-held desire) to come into my life, in the name of Jesus.

30. Divine Favor, fast track the manifestation of _____ (long-held desire) in my life, in the name of Jesus.

31. _____ (long-held desire), let Your arrival be brought forward speedily, in the name of Jesus.

32. _____ (long-held desire), arrive sooner into my life rather than later, in the name of Jesus.

33. As it happened for Abraham and Sarah, whose wait finally came to an end, my wait concerning my long-held desires, come to an end now, in the name of Jesus.

34. Thank You because I know that You have heard me and I will soon testify of Your favor and goodness upon my life, in the name of Jesus.

35. Thank You Lord for regarding my prayers and for answering them, in Jesus' mighty name, amen.

CHAPTER 20

FAVOR THAT PREVENTS DESOLATION

"Now therefore, O our God, hear the prayer of thy servant, and his supplications, and cause thy face to shine upon thy sanctuary that is desolate, for the Lord's sake." — Daniel 9:17 (KJV)

PURPOSE

This prayer session is:

- To prevent or end social, emotional, spiritual or any other kind of desolation
- To unleash an era of love, warmth and community in your life

PRAYERS

1. Yahweh, I am the object of Your goodwill, therefore, I will not live a bleak life, in the name of Jesus.

2. Give your grace unto me, O Lord, and let every manifestation of emptiness in my life be terminated, in the name of Jesus.

3. I want any damage that my life has suffered to be repaired. Give ear to my prayers, O Lord, and cause Your repair work in my life to begin, in the name of Jesus.

4. Let me obtain favor from You, Everlasting Father. And by reason of Your favor, protect me from any manifestation of unhappiness or sadness, in the name of Jesus.

5. My Father, consider me today and rid me of any manifestation of loneliness, in the name of Jesus.

6. Have compassion on me, Jehovah, and shield me from any feeling of wretchedness, in the name of Jesus.

7. Be gracious unto me, Eternal king and do not let me experience untimely loss or sorrow in my life, in the name of Jesus.

8. I am a candidate of the kindness of the Most High God, therefore, there shall be no barrenness of any kind in my life, in the name of Jesus.

9. Elohim, since You know me by name, may I never be devoid of Your warmth and of the warmth of others, in the name of Jesus.

10. Lion of Judah, let me find grace in Your sight and let Your grace drive gloominess away from my life, in the name of Jesus.

11. O my Father, make Your face shine upon me and let me never be forsaken by You or by those who matter to me, in the name of Jesus.

12. Turn Your face toward me, O Lord, and cause any unpleasantness in my to depart, in the name of Jesus.

13. Messiah, be favorable unto me and let Your favor crush any stone of abandonment that may have been designed to weigh me down, in the name of Jesus.

14. Sanctifier, let me find favor with You and let Your favor prevent me from being left out of anything I am eligible for, in the name of Jesus.

15. Redeemer, target me with Your grace and let Your grace shield me from any kind of grief or bitterness of heart, in the name of Jesus.

16. Help me O Lord and with Your help, may I never be neglected, in the name of Jesus.

17. Help me O Lord, and with Your help, may I never be shunned by those who matter to me, in the name of Jesus.

18. My Father in heaven, shower we with Your favor so that I can never be an outcast, in the name of Jesus.

19. By reason of God's love upon me, may I never be ditched, in the name of Jesus.

20. God forbids it that I be disregarded by anyone or any place that matters to me, in the name of Jesus.

21. Abba Father, may I never be dropped by those who matter to me, in the name of Jesus.

22. The pain of being ignored by those who matter to a person shall never again be my pain, in the name of Jesus.

23. The divine favor of God is upon my life, therefore, I shall be cherished by those who matter to me, in the name of Jesus.

24. God mandates it that people will seek me out to befriend me, in the name of Jesus.

25. The kindness of God in my life shall be the fountain of my happiness, in the name of Jesus.

26. Divine Favor confers on me God's divine perfume which causes me to be appealing to everyone especially those that matter to me, in the name of Jesus.

27. I have obtained the favor of God, therefore, **I am loved**, in the name of Jesus.

28. I have obtained the favor of God, therefore, **I shall benefit from His support and that of others**, in the name of Jesus.

29. I have obtained the favor of God, therefore, **I shall be helped by Him and by others**, in the name of Jesus.

30. I have obtained the favor of God, therefore, **I am mandated to be helpful to others**, in the name of Jesus.

31. I have obtained the favor of God, therefore, **I am nurtured by God and by others**, in the name of Jesus.

32. I have obtained the favor of God, therefore, **my life is filled with meaning**, in the name of Jesus.

33. I have obtained the favor of God, therefore, **my life is filled with joy**, in the name of Jesus.

34. I have obtained the favor of God, therefore, **my life is filled with optimism**, in the name of Jesus.

35. I have obtained the favor of God, therefore, **I am hopeful**, in the name of Jesus.

36. I have obtained the favor of God, therefore, **I am relevant to people**, in the name of Jesus.

37. I have obtained the favor of God, therefore, **I am important to others**, in the name of Jesus.

38. I have obtained the favor of God, therefore, **I am of good cheer**, in the name of Jesus.

39. I have obtained the favor of God, therefore, **I am encouraged**, in the name of Jesus.

40. I have obtained the favor of God, therefore, **I am enthusiastic**, in the name of Jesus.

41. I have obtained the favor of God, therefore, **prosperity is my portion**, in the name of Jesus.

42. I have obtained the favor of God, therefore, **I am complete and whole**, in the name of Jesus.

43. Thank You Father for Your favor in answering these prayers of mine, in Jesus' mighty name, amen.

CHAPTER 21
FAVOR FOR JOYFUL EMOTIONS

"For his anger endureth but a moment; in his favour is life: weeping may endure for a night, but joy cometh in the morning." — Psalm 30:5 (KJV)

PURPOSE

This prayer session is:

- For the banishment of negative emotions
- For the manifestation of Joy and other positive feelings

PRAYERS

1. Jehovah Jireh, You are my provider. Answer my prayers today and let positivity be released into my life, in the name of Jesus.

2. Hand of God, banish **misery** from my life, in the name of Jesus.

3. Favor of God, bring **bliss** into my life, in the name of Jesus.

4. Hand of God, banish **agony** from my life, in the name of Jesus.

5. Favor of God, draw **enjoyment** into my life, in the name of Jesus.

6. Hand of God, banish **dejection** from my life, in the name of Jesus.

7. Favor of God, draw **jubilation** into my life, in the name of Jesus.

8. Hand of God, banish **gloominess** from my life, in the name of Jesus.

9. Favor of God, bring **smiles** into my life, in the name of Jesus.

10. Hand of God, banish **despair** from my life, in the name of Jesus.

11. Favor of God, bring **laughter** into my life, in the name of Jesus.

12. Hand of God, banish **sadness** from my life, in the name of Jesus.

13. Favor of God, bring **lightheartedness** into my life, in the name of Jesus.

14. Hand of God, banish **sorrow** from my life, in the name of Jesus.

15. Favor of God, *take me to the top of the world with joy*, in the name of Jesus.

16. Hand of God, banish **depression** from my life, in the name of Jesus.

17. Favor of God, make me feel **accomplished** and **whole**, in the name of Jesus.

18. Hand of God, banish **woes** from my life, in the name of Jesus.

19. Favor of God, bring **serenity** into my life, in the name of Jesus.

20. Hand of God, banish **frustrations** from my life, in the name of Jesus.

21. Favor of God, bring **prosperity** into my life, in the name of Jesus.

22. Hand of God, banish **failure** from life, in the name of Jesus.

23. Favor of God, bring **success** into my life, in the name of Jesus.

24. Hand of God, banish **sickness** and **disease** from my life, in the name of Jesus.

25. Favor of God, bring **good health** into my life, in the name of Jesus.

26. Hand of God, banish **worry** from my life, in the name of Jesus.

27. Favor of God, bring **calmness** into my life, in the name of Jesus.

28. Hand of God, banish **heartbreaks** from my life, in the name of Jesus.

29. Favor of God, bring **happiness** into my life, in the name of Jesus.

30. Hand of God, banish **dissatisfaction** from my life, in the name of Jesus.

31. Favor of God, bring **contentment** into my life, in the name of Jesus.

32. Hand of God, banish **irritability** from my life, in the name of Jesus.

33. Favor of God, make me **easy-going**, in the name of Jesus.

34. Most High God, let Your face shine on me and let good fortune be my lot, in the name of Jesus.

35. Rock of Ages, turn Your face toward me and let me experience seasons of great pleasure throughout my lifetime, in the name of Jesus.

36. My Father in heaven, be gracious unto me and let there be shouts of rejoicing in my household, in the name of Jesus.

37. Righteous Father, let me find favor with You and let there be dancing in my household, in the name of Jesus.

38. The favor of the Lord brings uplifting into my life today. My glory shall be raised high and shall shine, in the name of Jesus.

39. The favor of the Lord fills me with joyful emotions today, in the name of Jesus.

40. The favor of the Lord causes others to bring joyful experiences into my life from today, in the name of Jesus.

41. The favor of the Lord empowers me to bring joy into the lives of others, in the name of Jesus.

42. Father, may I experience such goodness in this life that will give me cause to regularly jump for joy, in the name of Jesus.

43. Let there be regular joy jumps in my household, O Lord, by reason of Your blessing upon us, in the name of Jesus.

44. Lord, as You cause Your face to shine upon me, let the look of joy appear on my own face all the time, in the name of Jesus.

45. May I be continually filled with joy all the days of my life, in the name of Jesus.

46. Thank You Father God for Your great favor to me in answering my prayers, in Jesus' mighty name, amen.

CHAPTER 22

FAVOR FOR DIVINE ELEVATION

"For thou art the glory of their strength: and in thy favour our horn shall be exalted." — Psalm 89:17 (KJV)

PURPOSE

This prayer session is:

- For promotion in the workplace
- For general career upliftment
- For professional breakthroughs
- To break the backbone of stagnancy or backwardness
- For rescue from business degradation
- To experience an increase in work or business income

PRAYERS

1. I am a beneficiary of the kindness of Almighty God. Therefore, my case is different and it is for the best, in the name of Jesus.

2. Where others are being demoted, I shall receive profitable promotions, in the name of Jesus.

3. Where others are being downgraded, I shall experience dramatic increases in my professional level, in the name of Jesus.

4. Where others are being relegated, I shall be moved on to more important work, in the name of Jesus.

5. Where others are being downsized, I will be moved on to more fulfilling roles, in the name of Jesus.

6. Where others are being humiliated, I shall experience dramatic career growth, in the name of Jesus.

7. Where others may be stagnant, I shall experience exponential increase in my income, in the name of Jesus.

8. Where others may be dishonored, I shall enjoy increase in work responsibilities, in the name of Jesus.

9. Where others may be mediocre, the spirit of excellence shall be my portion, in the name of Jesus.

10. Where others may remain in obscurity, I shall receive more and more power to do good work, in the name of Jesus.

11. Where others may be hindered, my professional influence shall increase greatly, in the name of Jesus.

12. Where others may be blocked, I shall receive extraordinary support and backing so that I can keep making progress, in the name of Jesus.

13. Where others may be held back, I shall be boosted and uplifted by my superiors, in the name of Jesus.

14. Where others may be kept in check, I shall become a preferred candidate for rapid advancement, in the name of Jesus.

15. Where others may be oppressed, I shall be recognized for my good work and encouraged, in the name of Jesus.

16. Where others may be debased, I shall be pushed up the professional ladder unto greatness, in the name of Jesus.

17. Where others may be terminated, I shall be rewarded for my excellence, in the name of Jesus.

18. Where others may be canceled, I shall be honored for my illustriousness, in the name of Jesus.

19. If I run a business, divine favor will make it such that it shall receive sponsorship, in the name of Jesus.

20. If I run a business, it shall become a first class candidate for investment, in the name of Jesus.

21. My business shall be the beneficiary of countless endorsements, in the name of Jesus.

22. My business shall be the beneficiary of countless recommendations, in the name of Jesus.

23. Whatever my business is qualified to apply for, upon application, shall receive approval, in the name of Jesus.

24. Divine Favor will cause my business to explode for good and bring me financial breakthroughs, in the name of Jesus.

25. Lord, let all these things I have asked for be given unto me so that my life can be a shining example of the power of Your hand upon an ordinary human being who is faithful to You, in the name of Jesus.

26. Thank You Father God for answering my prayers, in Jesus' mighty name, amen.

CHAPTER 23

FAVOR FOR DUMBFOUNDING BREAKTHROUGH

"And delivered him out of all his afflictions, and gave him favour and wisdom in the sight of Pharaoh king of Egypt; and he made him governor over Egypt and all his house." — Acts 7:10 (KJV)

PURPOSE

This prayer session is:

- For the release of the Spirit of Excellence
- For the ability to create new things
- For the ability to create profitable things
- For whatever you create to bring the desired breakthrough

PRAYERS

1. I serve the Mighty God. Dumbfounding breakthroughs is my birthright, in the name of Jesus.

2. If Joseph could experience dumbfounding breakthrough, I will also experience it in my life, in the name of Jesus.

3. I am tired of setbacks, I want to move forward. O Lord, have mercy and make it happen for me, in the name of Jesus.

4. I am fed up of stagnancy. It's time for me to fulfill destiny. Lord God, stretch Your hand of favor toward me and make it happen for me, in the name of Jesus.

5. I do not want any more failure or any more disappointments. I need a breakthrough now. Lord, help me, in the name of Jesus.

6. I keep hoping and waiting for better days BUT now Lord, I want a change. Come to my rescue, in the name of Jesus.

7. Enough of the inactivity in my life. Lord, come to my rescue, in the name of Jesus.

8. Enough of the wishes and dreams. I want to act now to become somebody great in life. Lord, come to my aid, in the name of Jesus.

9. Enough of the lack of helpers or resources. Lord, You know all the helpers and You have all the resources. Favor me and hook me up into the breakthrough grid, in the name of Jesus.

10. Lord, cause Your face to shine upon me so that I can be ushered into my own season of breakthrough, in the name of Jesus.

11. Jehovah, let that exceptional spirit that was upon Joseph, enter into my life now to make me exceptional in this generation, in the name of Jesus.

12. Father, my life is open and available. Let the Spirit of excellence enter into my life and move me to do the unusual and the uncommon, in the name of Jesus.

13. My God, cause me to have an uncommon ability to understand and process information, in the name of Jesus.

14. King of kings, make me have uncommon insights into solutions for problems, in the name of Jesus.

15. Spirit of excellence, unleash in me the ability to innovate, in the name of Jesus.

16. Spirit of excellence, unleash in me the ability to refine and improve things that already exist, in the name of Jesus.

17. Spirit of excellence, provide me with mental suggestions and ideas that can unleash progress, in the name of Jesus.

18. Lord, let me have sudden realizations of profitable processes and methods, in the name of Jesus.

19. Elohim, give me the ability to manage a multitude of things without becoming overwhelmed, in the name of Jesus.

20. Help me Lord to move through obstacles no one has ever moved through before in order to achieve breakthrough, in the name of Jesus.

21. My Father and my God, show me Your favor so that I too can create something that helps humanity, in the name of Jesus.

22. By Your hand of favor upon me, O Lord, let me solve a very big problem and find out a way to profit from it, in the name of Jesus.

23. Almighty God, give me the ability to create new techniques from scratch, in the name of Jesus.

24. O God, give me the ability to create new products and services from scratch, in the name of Jesus.

25. Father God, have uncommon compassion on me and let me make something new that will be regarded as a groundbreaking achievement in my field, in the name of Jesus.

26. Holy Father, bless me with sudden and shocking opportunities that will unleash breakthroughs in my life, in the name of Jesus.

27. Eternal King, let whatever comes out of my hand create new recurring income sources for me, in the name of Jesus.

28. Father, never let me relent. Bless me with the knack to always want to discover new profit sources, in the name of Jesus.

29. The favor of the Lord will bring me recognition for whatever I create, in the name of Jesus.

30. Through the favor of God, may my creations make a name for me in my field and bring me renown, in the name of Jesus.

31. Through the favor of God in my life, and by reason of the force of my creations, wherever doors had been closed in my face, they shall begin to open, in the name of Jesus.

32. Product and service uniqueness shall be my portion, in the name of Jesus.

33. Unbelievable patronage shall be my portion, in he name of Jesus.

34. It is my time to shine and my season of breakthrough. The favor of the Lord will make me shine, in the name of Jesus.

35. Re-engineer me O Lord and fine-tune me to handle divinely-orchestrated breakthroughs, in the name of Jesus.

36. Thank You Father for answering my prayers, in Jesus' mighty name, amen.

CHAPTER 24

FAVOR FOR SECURITY IN TIMES OF TROUBLE

"O LORD, be gracious unto us; we have waited for thee: be thou their arm every morning, our salvation also in the time of trouble." — Isaiah 33:2 (KJV)

PURPOSE

This prayer session is:

- For security in times of trouble
- For divine protection against human and spiritual harm
- To have peace of mind, come what may

PRAYERS

1. O Lord, as I make my prayers unto You in this session, be gracious unto me and answer them, in the name of Jesus.

2. Jehovah Shalom, You are the one who brings salvation in times of trouble. Come and bring Your salvation into my life today, in the name of Jesus.

3. Father, there are people out there, who for reasons best known to them, may be planning a physical attack against me. Consider me and save me from any kind of physical attack, in the name of Jesus.

4. Everlasting Father, today, I invite You to come watch over me to keep me safe in times of trouble, in the name of Jesus.

5. I Am that I Am, give Your grace unto me and protect me from demonic planners of spiritual attacks against me, in the name of Jesus.

6. Great God, look upon me with Your favor and secure my life. Let all my exposures to evil attacks be closed down, in the name of Jesus.

7. My God, let all my vulnerabilities to all forms of attacks be discovered and blocked, in the name of Jesus.

8. Eternal King, let me find favor in Your sight and let all the wide open security gates of my life be shut, to keep me safe, in the name of Jesus.

9. Merciful Father, hide me under Your shadow so that the wickedness of man and of the devil will not reach me, in the name of Jesus.

10. Lord of hosts, keep me safe from injury, in the name of Jesus.

11. Lord of lords, may my blood not be shed by reason of an attack against me, in the name of Jesus.

12. Have compassion on me Emmanuel. Whenever trouble comes towards me, cover me, so that it will not touch me, in the name of Jesus.

13. Benevolent God, shield me from all forms of danger, in the name of Jesus.

14. Benevolent God, defend me from all those who call themselves my enemies, in the name of Jesus.

15. Let all the evil imaginations of my enemies against me come to nothing, in the name of Jesus.

16. Father, I am a candidate of Your kindness, protect me from loss, in the name of Jesus.

17. Lord, I am a beneficiary of Your compassion, protect me against all fatalities, in the name of Jesus.

18. Now Lord, by reason of Your favor, may all curses issued against me come to nothing, in the name of Jesus.

19. By reason of the favor of the Lord, all spells designed against me shall come to nothing, in the name of Jesus.

20. All jinxes prepared against me shall come to nothing, in the name of Jesus.

21. All evil wishes projected against me shall come to nothing, in the name of Jesus.

22. Favor of God, arise, and let all evil arrows fired against me by evil priests, return to sender, in the name of Jesus.

23. Favor of God, arise and let all pronouncements issued against me by witchdoctors, return to sender, in the name of Jesus.

24. Favor of God, arise, and shield me against demonic visitations, in the name of Jesus.

25. Because I have the favor of God in my life, I will never fall into any pit dug for me by my enemies, in the name of Jesus.

26. Workplace pits, I am not your candidate, I shall not fall into you, in the name of Jesus.

27. Business pits, I am not your candidate, I shall not fall into you, in the name of Jesus.

28. Financial pits, I am not your candidate, I shall not fall into you, in the name of Jesus.

29. Relationship pits, I am not your candidate, I shall not fall into you, in the name of Jesus.

30. Emotional pits, I am not your candidate, I shall not fall into you, in the name of Jesus.

31. Marital pits, I am not your candidate, I shall not fall into you, in the name of Jesus.

32. Spiritual pits, I am not your candidate, I shall not fall into you, in the name of Jesus.

33. Father, be favorable unto me and make me untouchable by the enemy, in the name of Jesus.

34. Great Redeemer, be favorable unto me, make me unmovable by the enemy, in the name of Jesus.

35. O Lord I pray, make me unshakable by the enemy, in the name of Jesus.

36. Messiah, make me unshatterable by the enemy, in the name of Jesus.

37. Since I am the object of Your goodwill O God, build me to last the test of times, in the name of Jesus.

38. Since You know me by name, O Lord, let me live a life free from worries about the activities of my enemies, in the name of Jesus.

39. Lord, let me live free from fear, in the name of Jesus.

40. Holy Father, let me live free from anxiety, in the name of Jesus.

41. My Father in heaven, let me live free from insecurities, in the name of Jesus.

42. I am favored of the Lord, therefore, I shall be established in the peace that He provides for me, in the name of Jesus.

43. Thank You Father God for You great favor in answering my prayers in this session, in Jesus' mighty name, amen.

CHAPTER 25

FAVOR FOR FINDING A LIFE PARTNER

"Whoso findeth a wife findeth a good thing, and obtaineth favour of the LORD."
— Proverbs 18:22 (KJV)

PURPOSE

This prayer session is:

- For locating your life partner
- For getting married as soon as possible

PRAYERS

1. My Redeemer, one of the greatest favors You can do for me is to help me find my destined life partner. Therefore, Father, on this issue, You have to turn Your face to me and favor me, in the name of Jesus.

2. Almighty God, I do not want to make the wrong choice. Come to my aid and help me choose right, in the name of Jesus.

3. Lord, I know that choosing wrong may even cause me to land myself in hell fire. Help me to find a spouse with whom I can succeed on earth as a married person and with whom I can make heaven, in the name of Jesus.

4. My God, I am tired of being single. Help get me married, in the name of Jesus.

5. Lord, I do not want to remain unmarried any longer. Help me get me married, in the name of Jesus.

6. Since I have declared my desire to You O Lord, touch me with Your great hand so that I can benefit of Your kind favor in this issue of my marriage, in the name of Jesus.

7. May I never be in the wrong place to find a partner, in the name of Jesus.

8. May I never be in the right place but at the wrong time to find a partner, in the name of Jesus.

9. May I never overlook the right person for me, in the name of Jesus.

10. Father, when the right person and I are in close proximity, may I never pass them by, in the name of Jesus.

11. Any spirit of lust assigned to divert me away from God's purpose for my life, my life is not your candidate. Depart from me and never return, in the name of Jesus.

12. If I am invited to a place where my destined partner is, may I not skip such an invitation, in the name of Jesus.

13. If I should encounter my destined partner, may I never disregard them for any reason, in the name of Jesus.

14. May I never ignore my destined partner, in the name of Jesus.

15. If I am already in a friendship with my destined partner, Favor of God, open my eyes to realize God's plan for me, in the name of Jesus.

16. May I never let go of God's plan for me, in the name of Jesus.

17. Have compassion on me O Lord on the issue of marriage. Give me opportunities to encounter my destined partner, in the name of Jesus.

18. On the day that I shall encounter my life partner, may I be ready, in the name of Jesus.

19. On the day that I encounter my life partner, may I not fall short before them, in the name of Jesus.

20. May I not make a bad first impression on my destined partner, in the name of Jesus.

21. Have mercy O Lord. Even if I make a bad first impression, may I be given more opportunities with my destined partner to make better impressions, in the name of Jesus.

22. May I never bypass my destined lover, in the name of Jesus.

23. May I never blow off my destined life partner, in the name of Jesus.

24. Father Lord, may my ignorance not cause me to run away from the person You have destined for me, in the name of Jesus.

25. Help me O Lord so that I can happen upon my destined partner serendipitously, in the name of Jesus.

26. Holy One of Israel, use whatever means You choose to help me get to know of or about the lover of my dreams, in the name of Jesus.

27. Eternal God, help me to discover my destined partner, in the name of Jesus.

28. Lead me O Lord to wherever I need to go in order to encounter the person You have assigned for me from the foundation of the universe, in the name of Jesus.

29. Lord, since I am the object of Your goodwill, let me locate my life partner, in the name of Jesus.

30. If it be Your will, O Lord, let me stumble upon my destined partner wherever and whenever You choose, in the name of Jesus.

31. You created me Father. You already know my future. Therefore, this very year, let me turn up at whatever place my life partner will be so I can meet them, in the name of Jesus.

32. This very year, the divine favor of God will cause me to catch sight of my destined partner so I can make my move and close this chapter of my life, in the name of Jesus.

33. King of kings, have mercy on me and make my life easier. Reveal to me my destined partner using any means You desire, in the name of Jesus.

34. Jehovah, use a friend to reveal my destined partner to me, in the name of Jesus.

35. Lord, use my family members to reveal my destined partner to me, in the name of Jesus.

36. O God, use my colleagues to reveal my destined partner to me, in the name of Jesus.

37. Father, use whomever or whatever You desire to make my dreams come true, in the name of Jesus.

38. Because I have the favor of God upon my life, I too shall have a helpmate, in the name of Jesus.

39. Because of the favor of God, I too shall have a soulmate, in the name of Jesus.

40. I too shall have a better half, in the name of Jesus.

41. I too shall have a life partner, in the name of Jesus.

42. I too shall have a lifelong lover, in the name of Jesus.

43. I too shall have a best friend, in the name of Jesus.

44. I too shall have a destiny companion, in the name of Jesus.

45. God willing, I shall marry, in the name of Jesus.

46. God willing, I shall tie the knot, in the name of Jesus.

47. Because the Lord is gracious unto me, soonest, I too shall walk down the isle, in the name of Jesus.

48. Since the Lord knows me by name, I too shall be joined in matrimony with my destined partner, in the name of Jesus.

49. As the Lord liveth, soonest, I shall exit the single life and settle down with my destined partner to the glory of God, in the name of Jesus.

50. Thank You O Lord for Your great favor to me in answering my prayers, in Jesus' mighty name, amen.

CHAPTER 26

FAVOR FOR PROPERTY ACQUISITION

"For they got not the land in possession by their own sword, neither did their own arm save them: but thy right hand, and thine arm, and the light of thy countenance, because thou hadst a favour unto them."
— Psalm 44:3 (KJV)

PURPOSE

This prayer session is:

- For divine favor to claim whatever belongs to you
- To become completely dependent on God for everything
- For becoming a property owner during your lifetime through God's help

PRAYERS

1. Great Provider, if You have allotted anything to me in this life, I must possess it, it will be mine, in the name of Jesus.

2. My King and my God, I know that I can only have what You give to me. So I ask: Give to me what You have allocated to me, in the name of Jesus.

3. Like the Israelites, I know that my efforts alone can not take me where I want to go. So, my Father, come and help me get there, in the name of Jesus.

4. Most High God, You used Your right hand to help the Israelites. Favor me and use Your right hand to help me as well, in the name of Jesus.

5. Eternal Father, You used Your arm to help the children of Israel. Deploy Your mighty arm for my sake also, in the name of Jesus.

6. Great and Mighty God, You used the light of Your countenance to help the Hebrews. Let me benefit from the light of Your countenance today, in the name of Jesus.

7. Because You favored the Israelites, they possessed their possession. Father, favor me so that I too can possess my possessions, in the name of Jesus.

8. Christ Jesus my Lord, I am tired of being a tenant. Favor me so that I can become a landlord, in the name of Jesus.

9. By thy right hand O Lord, let me move from being a renter to an owner, in the name of Jesus.

10. By thy right hand O Lord, let me move from being a guest to a host, in the name of Jesus.

11. By thy right hand O Lord, let me move from being a wisher to a builder, in the name of Jesus.

12. By thy right hand O Lord, let me move from being a dreamer to a fulfilled occupant of my own house, in the name of Jesus.

13. Father, let Your strong arm help me to obtain my own assets, in the name of Jesus.

14. Everlasting Father, let Your strong arm help me to buy my own properties, in the name of Jesus.

15. Light of the World, let Your strong arm help me to take possession of my own properties in this life, in the name of Jesus.

16. Elohim, let Your strong arm help me to control my own properties, in the name of Jesus.

17. The strong arm of the Lord shall help me stand in the committee of property owners, in the name of Jesus.

18. Light of God's countenance, shine upon me. Make me a person who owns land, in the name of Jesus.

19. Light of God's countenance, shine upon me. Make me a person who rents out land, in the name of Jesus.

20. Light of God's countenance, shine upon me. Make me a person who owns apartments, in the name of Jesus.

21. Light of God's countenance, shine upon me. Make me a person who rents out apartments, in the name of Jesus.

22. Light of God's countenance, shine upon me. Make me a person who owns whole buildings, in the name of Jesus.

23. Light of God's countenance, shine upon me. Make me a person who rents out whole buildings, in the name of Jesus.

24. Light of God's countenance, shine upon me. Let people from diverse backgrounds pay me for the privilege of living in my buildings, in the name of Jesus.

25. Light of God's countenance, shine upon me so that I can live in my own apartment or building, in the name of Jesus.

26. Light of God's countenance, shine upon me so I can experience building houses from scratch over and over as I build my own portfolio, in the name of Jesus.

27. Light of God's countenance, shine upon me so I can become a buyer and seller of houses, in the name of Jesus.

28. Soonest, I shall be called a landlord, in the name of Jesus.

29. Soonest, I shall be called a lessor, in the name of Jesus.

30. Soonest, I shall be called a real estate mogul, in the name of Jesus.

31. Soonest, I shall be an established owner of properties ONLY because the Lord is helping me, in the name of Jesus.

32. Thank You O Lord for Your favor in answering these prayers of mine, in Jesus' mighty name, amen.

CHAPTER 27

FAVOR FOR PEACE WITH ENEMIES

"When a man's ways please the LORD, he maketh even his enemies to be at peace with him."
— Proverbs 16:7 (KJV)

PURPOSE

This prayer session is:

- For securing peace with your enemies, if you prefer
- For securing an environment conducive to success in life
- For the enjoyment of your life
- For divine judgment against unrepentant enemies

PRAYERS

1. O Lord God Almighty, I am trying my best. Let my ways be pleasing to You, in the name of Jesus.

2. If there is anything in my life, O Lord, that You find unpleasant, I repent of it. Forgive me, in the name of Jesus.

3. Adonai, I need to concentrate on my destiny. Enemies can be distracting. Therefore, I need Your help to be at peace with them, in the name of Jesus.

4. Abba Father, let me find favor with You such that You will make my enemies to be at peace with me, in the name of Jesus.

5. El Elyon, I am tired of animosities. Favor me and make peace between me and my enemies, in the name of Jesus.

6. El Shaddai, I am tired of discord. Favor me and make peace between me and my enemies, in the name of Jesus.

7. I am fed up of conflicts. O Lord, favor me and make peace between me and my enemies, in the name of Jesus.

8. Jehovah, I am tired of feuds. Favor me and make peace between me and my enemies, in the name of Jesus.

9. Redeemer, I am fed up of tensions. Favor me and make peace between me and my enemies, in the name of Jesus.

10. Rock of Ages, I am tired of bad blood. Favor me and make peace between me and my enemies, in the name of Jesus.

11. Messiah, I am tired of altercations. Favor me and make peace between me and my enemies, in the name of Jesus.

12. O my Father, I am tired of constant fighting. Favor me and make peace between me and my enemies, in the name of Jesus.

13. O my Lord, I am tired of strife. Favor me and make peace between me and my enemies, in the name of Jesus.

14. My Shepherd, I am tired of pandemonium. Favor me and make peace between me and my enemies, in the name of Jesus.

15. I am tired of being distracted from my destiny assignment by these enemies. My God, favor me and make peace between me and my enemies, in the name of Jesus.

16. If I have found favor with You O Lord, let all physical attacks or plans of physical attacks against me be halted, in the name of Jesus.

17. O God, declare a truce between me and my foes, in the name of Jesus.

18. Father, let there be a de-escalation between me and my adversaries, in the name of Jesus.

19. Almighty God, intervene to strike an accord with my attackers so I can have peace, in the name of Jesus.

20. King of kings, let there be harmony between me and my opponents, in the name of Jesus.

21. Lord of lords, cause a cessation of hostilities between me and my challengers, in the name of Jesus.

22. Lord of hosts, create tranquility between me and my competitors, in the name of Jesus.

23. Prince of peace, declare a truce between me and my rivals, in the name of Jesus.

24. Merciful God, declare a truce between me and my detractors, in the name of Jesus.

25. Everlasting father, let the guns go silent between me and any kind of enemy, in the name of Jesus.

26. Activate Your favor in my, O Lord, and give me freedom from disturbance, in the name of Jesus.

27. Switch on Your favor in my life, O Lord, so I can live without conflict, in the name of Jesus.

28. Father, let Your favor afford me quietness of mind, in the name of Jesus.

29. Mighty God, let Your favor deliver me from oppressive thoughts about my enemies, in the name of Jesus.

30. Lord, let me enjoy a life without the constant pressure of enemies, in the name of Jesus.

31. Favor of God, arise, and create co-existence between me and my enemies without disagreement, in the name of Jesus.

32. Favor of God, arise, and give me freedom from the noise of enemies, in the name of Jesus.

33. Favor of God, arise, and give me freedom from worrying about enemies, in the name of Jesus.

34. Favor of God, arise and give me freedom from anxiety, in the name of Jesus.

35. Favor of God, arise, and give me freedom from strife, in the name of Jesus.

36. Favor of God, arise, and give me freedom from wasting my resources on protection against enemies, in the name of Jesus.

37. Favor of God, arise, and give me freedom from the public disgrace of fighting, in the name of Jesus.

38. Favor of God, arise, and save me from the reputation damage that comes with conflict, in the name of Jesus.

39. Favor of God, arise, and save me from the health challenges that may come from constantly engaging with enemies, in the name of Jesus.

40. Have mercy on me, O Lord, so I can live in a trouble-free state, in the name of Jesus.

41. Be merciful unto me O God so I can live in a stress-free state, in the name of Jesus.

42. Holy Father, create allowance for rapport between me and my enemies, in the name of Jesus.

43. My God, let this rapport give me the allowance I need to make rapid progress, in the name of Jesus.

44. May my opposers become my supporters, in the name of Jesus.

45. May those hostile against me become friendly toward me, in the name of Jesus.

46. May my antagonists become protagonists in the story of my life, in the name of Jesus.

47. May people seeking to harm me become my protectors, in the name of Jesus.

48. May people who hate me become fans of mine, in the name of Jesus.

49. May those who are unhappy with my progress begin to rejoice at my growth, in the name of Jesus.

50. May those who have tried to halt my progress become accelerators of my destiny, in the name of Jesus,

51. May those who want vengeance against me develop sympathy and affection for me, in the name of Jesus.

52. May my aggressive competitors become my associates, in the name of Jesus.

53. May my great enemies become great friends, in the name of Jesus.

54. May my formidable enemies become great allies, in the name of Jesus.

55. May my bitter enemies become good comrades, in the name of Jesus.

56. May my sworn enemies become my avowed defenders, in the name of Jesus.

57. Now Lord, if there be any kind of enemy who resists making peace with me, by the power of Your Holy Spirit who resides in me, I arrest that enemy and hand them over to You for divine judgment. Do with them as You please, in the name of Jesus.

58. Great and Mighty God, keep me safe from the devil and his demons who can never be at peace with me. Never let their power succeed over me, in the name of Jesus.

59. Father, be gracious unto me so that my ways can continue to please You and so that I can continue to enjoy peace with my enemies, in the name of Jesus.

60. Thank You Great God for answering my prayers in this session, in Jesus' mighty name, amen.

CHAPTER 28

FAVOR FOR A GREAT NAME

"And I will make of thee a great nation, and I will bless thee, and make thy name great; and thou shalt be a blessing" — Genesis 12:2 (KJV)

PURPOSE

This prayer session is:

- To avoid living an ordinary life
- For living a life of honor based on accomplishments
- For the establishment of your name on the earth

PRAYERS

1. I want to be blessed. Bless me, O Lord, in the name of Jesus.

2. I want my name to be great. Make my name great, O Lord, in the name of Jesus.

3. I want to be a blessing unto others. Make me a blessing, O Lord, in the name of Jesus.

4. I want to have great descendants. Help me, O Lord and make this my reality, in the name of Jesus.

5. I reject a dishonorable existence. This shall not be my portion, in the name of Jesus.

6. I do not want to live an uninspiring life, O Lord. Touch me with Your hand of favor and transform my life for good, in the name of Jesus.

7. My God, I hate living an inferior life. Have mercy on me and transform my life, in the name of Jesus.

8. Messiah, a mediocre can never have a great name. Deliver me from any spirit of mediocrity that may be living inside of me, in the name of Jesus.

9. Great Deliverer, I do not want to live a life that I will look back on and see that it is of no significance. Invade my space today, Lord, and change things for better for me, in the name of Jesus.

10. I reject a substandard existence. O Lord, intervene and set me on a new trajectory, in the name of Jesus.

11. I reject an average life. O Lord, arise and deliver me from the spirit of average, in the name of Jesus.

12. Lord, I am fed up with feeling inadequate all the time. Come Lord and make a change in my life today, in the name of Jesus.

13. My God, I am tired of spending my time on worthless ventures. Come and rescue me today, so I can spend my life on things that matter, in the name of Jesus.

14. Alpha and Omega, deliver me from any spirit and trait of incompetence that may be in my life, in the name of Jesus.

15. My Shepherd, I need to become deep. I am tired of living a shallow life. Come and add depth to my life, in the name of Jesus.

16. If I have been unserious all my life, O Lord, I apologize. I need to turn a new leaf. Let me find favor in Your sight so that I can have a new beginning, in the name of Jesus.

17. Father, be kind to me. Make me into a principled person, in the name of Jesus.

18. Benevolent God, make me an upright person, in the name of Jesus.

19. Generous God, make me into a trustworthy person, in the name of Jesus.

20. Altruistic God, make me into a dependable person, in the name of Jesus.

21. Make me, O Lord, into someone that can be counted upon to deliver, in the name of Jesus.

22. Father, stretch Your helping hand to me and make me a faithful person, in the name of Jesus.

23. Lord, let Your favor upon my life begin to create positive changes in me that everyone can see, in the name of Jesus.

24. By Your divine power, my God, let me begin to do a variety of positive things that I have never done before, in the name of Jesus.

25. My Father and my God create changes in me that will cause me to be regarded with respect, in the name of Jesus.

26. Let Your favor arise in my life, Jehovah, and make me deserving of the respect of others, in the name of Jesus.

27. Jehovah, let Your favor arise in my life and cause me to become appreciated by those who matter, in the name of Jesus.

28. Favor of God, arise, and help me be in good standing with people, in the name of Jesus.

29. Favor of God, arise, and help me become a symbol of distinction, in the name of Jesus.

30. Favor of God, arise, and help me become an object of admiration, in the name of Jesus.

31. Favor of God, arise, and help me become a magnet of special recognition, in the name of Jesus.

32. Favor of God, arise, make me a person of unquestionable character, in the name of Jesus.

33. Favor of God, arise, and cause me to record remarkable achievements in my life, in the name of Jesus.

34. Favor of God, arise, and cause me to have a reputation for honesty, in the name of Jesus.

35. Favor of God, arise, and cause me to be renowned for fairness, in the name of Jesus.

36. Everlasting Father, create in me a willingness to stick to righteous principles, no matter what, in the name of Jesus.

37. Create in me, O Lord, a willingness to make sacrifices in order to set good examples, in the name of Jesus.

38. Favor of God, cause people to desire to associate with me, in the name of Jesus.

39. Favor of God, cause people to desire to be affiliated with my name, in the name of Jesus.

40. Let it be, O Lord, that someday soon, people will seek my endorsement because of the power and weight of my good name, in the name of Jesus.

41. Because You shall make my name great, O God, let unimaginable doors begin to open to me, in the name of Jesus.

42. May my name command attention, in the name of Jesus.

43. May my name command action, in the name of Jesus.

44. May my name always ring bells of glory, in the name of Jesus.

45. May my name elicit compassion, in the name of Jesus.

46. May my name elicit fondness in the hearts of people, in the name of Jesus.

47. By reason of the favor of the Lord upon my life, may I be counted amongst the privileged, in the name of Jesus.

48. Because of God's favor upon my life, I shall have a good track record throughout my life. God's favor shall also see to it that I shall have a record of impact on the lives of others, in the name of Jesus.

49. By the grace of God, may my name inspire the boys and men, girls and women of our world for generation unto generation to the glory of God, in the name of Jesus.

50. Thank You Excellency for answering my prayers, in Jesus' mighty name, amen.

CHAPTER 29

FAVOR FOR PROTECTION AGAINST FAILURE

"And if thou deal thus with me, kill me, I pray thee, out of hand, if I have found favour in thy sight; and let me not see my wretchedness." — Numbers 11:15 (KJV)

PURPOSE

This prayer session is:

- For protection against all forms of failure

PRAYERS

1. Lord, make Your face shine upon me and let me have victory over failure today, in the name of Jesus.

2. Father, I understand that there is no success without failure. But, the failure that never leads to success, that shall not be my portion any longer, in the name of Jesus.

3. Any voice of darkness asking me to quit and give up. I command you to be silent now and forever, in the name of Jesus.

4. Any spirit of weakness and inability to achieve set goals, my life is not your candidate. Depart now and never return, in the name of Jesus.

5. Hard work without success, I am not your candidate. Get out of my life now and forever, in the name of Jesus.

6. Evil powers that undo and cancel success, my life is not your candidate. I bind you with fetters and I cast you out of my life now, in the name of Jesus.

7. O my God, may I always give my all to whatever work lies before me, in the name of Jesus.

8. Poor performance, depart from my life, in the name of Jesus.

9. Spirit of lethargy on the platform of success, depart from my life and never return, in the name of Jesus.

10. From today, may I never fall short on the platform of opportunity, in the name of Jesus.

11. Help me O Lord to always deliver when the opportunity to deliver is presented to me, in the name of Jesus.

12. Father, may I not become a spectator in my own show, in the name of Jesus.

13. Evil voices telling me to rest when success is just ahead of me, be silenced now and forever, in the name of Jesus.

14. Any power of the enemy projecting tiredness into my life when my task is almost completed, I bind you and I cast you out of my life, in the name of Jesus.

15. Spirit of paralysis targeting me on the day of my performance, you have failed. Return to sender, in the name of Jesus.

16. My day of performance shall be my day of celebration, in the name of Jesus.

17. Dark powers that want to cancel my previous achievements, your time is up. I banish you from my life now, in the name of Jesus.

18. May the voice of my deficiencies not be louder than the voice of my capabilities on the day of my glory, in the name of Jesus.

19. Any spirit of dullness assigned to prevent me from understanding tasks which have been assigned to me, and which will determine my promotion, listen to me, I am not your candidate. I bind you and I cast you out, in the name of Jesus.

20. I will always live up to and exceed all the expectations that people have of me, in the name of Jesus.

21. Have compassion on me, O God, and cause me to never disappoint those who trust me, in the name of Jesus.

22. Have mercy O Lord, and deliver me from any voice telling me that my efforts will always be insufficient, in the name of Jesus.

23. Spirit of failure manifesting as weakness, depart from my life and never return, in the name of Jesus.

24. Spirit of failure manifesting as propensity to fall short, depart from me and never return, in the name of Jesus.

25. Spirit of failure manifesting as coming short in tests and exams, come out of my life permanently and never return, in the name of Jesus.

26. O Lord, You know me by name, do not let the enemy have the final say about my life, in the name of Jesus.

27. May I never be a flop, in the name of Jesus.

28. May I never be a letdown, in the name of Jesus.

29. May I never be a non-achiever, in the name of Jesus.

30. May I never be incompetent, in the name of Jesus.

31. May I never be regarded as a mistake by those who put their trust in me, in the name of Jesus.

32. May I never be negligent, in the name of Jesus.

33. May I never be known for omissions in my work, in the name of Jesus.

34. May I never be labeled careless by the powers that be, in the name of Jesus.

35. May I never be labeled as irresponsible, in the name of Jesus.

36. May the spirit of failure not have the best of me, in the name of Jesus.

37. Lord, let me find grace in Your eyes and let me rise about failure, in the name of Jesus.

38. Favor of God, cause me to to rise above the negative conclusions of people concerning me, in the name of Jesus.

39. Favor of God, arise, and bless me with competence, in the name of Jesus.

40. Favor of God, arise, and bless me with proficiency, in the name of Jesus.

41. Favor of God, arise, and bless me with capability, in the name of Jesus.

42. Favor of God, arise, and bless me with success, in the name of Jesus.

43. Favor of God, arise, and bless me with accomplishments, in the name of Jesus.

44. Favor of God, arise, and bless me with achievements, in the name of Jesus.

45. Give Your grace to me O God, and let me always finish whatever I start, in the name of Jesus.

46. Give Your grace to me, heavenly Father, and let me always achieve results on anything I lay my hands on, in the name of Jesus.

47. Favor of God, let me go from failure to success, in the name of Jesus.

48. Favor of God, let me go from losing to winning, in the name of Jesus.

49. I shall grow from strength to strength because the Lord is with me, in the name of Jesus.

50. The kindness of God shall make me profitable, in the name of Jesus.

51. The benevolence of the Almighty shall make me prosperous, in the name of Jesus.

52. Because I am in the center of God's will, progress and triumph will always be my lot, in the name of Jesus.

53. Thank You Father for answering my prayers, in Jesus' mighty name, amen.

CHAPTER 30

FAVOR FOR GENERAL WELL-BEING

"LORD, by thy favour thou hast made my mountain to stand strong..." — Psalm 30:7 (KJV)

PURPOSE

This prayer session is:

- For your general well-being
- For good health
- For prosperity
- For happiness

PRAYERS

1. Jehovah Jireh, I want to be satisfied with the state of my life. Unleash Your favor upon my life so that my desire can be granted, in the name of Jesus.

2. By Your favor, Lord, let me enjoy comfort in my time here on earth, in the name of Jesus.

3. By Your favor, Lord, give me good health, in the name of Jesus.

4. By Your favor, O God, let me enjoy happiness, in the name of Jesus.

5. By Your favor, O God, make me a beneficiary of prosperity, in the name of Jesus.

6. By Your favor, O Lord, let me have emotional well-being, in the name of Jesus.

7. By Your favor, O Lord, let me have physical well-being, in the name of Jesus.

8. By Your favor, O God, let me enjoy spiritual well-being, in the name of Jesus.

9. By Your favor, Holy Father, let me experience and enjoy economic well-being, in the name of Jesus.

PRAYERS FOR GOOD HEALTH

10. I reject sickness, in the name of Jesus.

11. Let Your favor keep me away from sickness, in the name of Jesus.

12. I shall not be bed-ridden, in the name of Jesus.

13. O Lord, keep me away from injury, in the name of Jesus.

14. I reject any form of anemia, in the name of Jesus.

15. Father, keep me in good physical condition, in the name of Jesus.

16. I reject mental disorder, in the name of Jesus.

17. Heavenly Father, let me enjoy good mental health, in the name of Jesus.

18. I reject any type of cancer, in the name of Jesus.

19. O Lord my God, shield my body from all diseases of the blood, in the name of Jesus.

20. I reject organ failure, in the name of Jesus.

21. I reject excess weight that leads to death, in the name of Jesus.

22. I reject overwork and stress that can make sick or kill, in the name of Jesus.

23. Stretch forth Your hand of support to me, O Lord and let me be given a sound mind, in the name of Jesus.

24. Give Your grace unto me, O Lord, and make my appearance fresh, in the name of Jesus.

25. Bless me with glowing skin, heavenly Father, that will testify to Your favor upon my life, in the name of Jesus.

26. By Your favor, O Lord, let me feel good and strong inside and outside, in the name of Jesus.

27. By reason of Your kindness to me, O Lord, let any test I take concerning my health return normal results, in the name of Jesus.

28. By Your favor, O Lord, let me always have the resources to afford healthy food and drink, in the name of Jesus.

29. Let Your favor, Father, always cause me to be attracted to reading wholesome content that will maintain my mental health, in the name of Jesus.

30. By Your favor, O Lord, may I always listen to content that will provoke me to think good thoughts and do good deeds, in the name of Jesus.

31. Let me never watch anything that will drive me to do evil, O God. Rather, let my interest always lie in seeing what will edify my life and move me forward, in the name of Jesus.

32. If I have found favor with You, O Lord, let me become physically sturdy and robust, in the name of Jesus.

33. Let me be physically active for as long as I shall live, in the name of Jesus,

34. Let me be bright-eyed all the days of my life, in the name of Jesus.

35. Let me be as fit as a fiddle for as long as I shall live, in the name of Jesus.

36. Favor of God, keep me well-conditioned, in the name of Jesus.

37. By Your favor, O God, cause me to always be in good shape, in the name of Jesus.

. . .

PRAYERS FOR HAPPINESS

38. Melancholy spirit without purpose, get out of my life now, in the name of Jesus.

39. Sadness spirit, get out of my life now, in the name of Jesus.

40. Spirit of depression, get out of my life now, in the name of Jesus.

41. Spirit of sorrow, my life is not your candidate. Get out now and never return, in the name of Jesus.

42. Spirit of negativity, get out of my life now, in the name of Jesus.

43. Spirit of despondency, get out of my life now, in the name of Jesus.

44. Spirit of unpleasantness, get out of my life now, in the name of Jesus.

45. Spirit of misfortune, out, out, out of my life now, in the name of Jesus.

46. Activate Your favor in my life, O Lord and let good things begin to happen in my life, in the name of Jesus.

47. Let me find grace in Your eyes, Father God, so that I can experience the goodness of life and feelings of pleasure, in the name of Jesus.

48. Let me find favor with You, O Lord, and make me a beneficiary of positive events, in the name of Jesus.

49. Father God, let Your favor bring contentment into my life, in the name of Jesus.

50. Messiah, let Your favor usher in times of delight into my life, in the name of Jesus.

51. King of kings, may Your favor upon me usher in happy times into my life, in the name of Jesus.

52. Favor of God, take me to a happy place, in the name of Jesus.

53. Be favorable unto me, Elohim. Let good things follow me such that feelings of good fortune will become my portion in life, in the name of Jesus.

54. By reason of the favor of God upon my life, let me always feel and tell myself that I am fortunate, in the name of Jesus.

55. God's hand of favor makes and keeps me positive, in the name of Jesus.

56. The hand of the Lord makes and keeps me cheerful, in the name of Jesus.

57. The hand of the Lord makes and keeps me joyful, in the name of Jesus.

58. The hand of the Lord makes and keeps me contented, in the name of Jesus.

59. The hand of the Lord makes and keeps me lively, in the name of Jesus.

60. The hand of the Lord makes and keeps me optimistic, in the name of Jesus.

61. The hand of the Lord makes and keeps me pleasant, in the name of Jesus.

62. The hand of the Lord makes and keeps me upbeat, in the name of Jesus.

63. The hand of the Lord makes and keeps me with nothing to complain about, in the name of Jesus.

PRAYERS FOR PROSPERITY

64. Favor of God, eject poverty from my life now, in the name of Jesus.

65. Favor of God, eject hardship from my life now, in the name of Jesus.

66. Favor of God, eject lack from my life now, in the name of Jesus.

67. Favor of God, eject frustration from my life now, in the name of Jesus.

68. Favor of God, eject begging from my life now, in the name of Jesus.

69. Favor of God, eject humiliation from my life now, in the name of Jesus.

70. Favor of God, eject financial paralysis from my life now, in the name of Jesus.

71. Favor of God, eject homelessness from my life now, in the name of Jesus.

72. Favor of God, eject shame from my life now, in the name of Jesus.

73. Favor of God, eject hunger from my life now, in the name of Jesus.

74. Favor of God, save me from the shame of still being a tenant in middle or old age, in the name of Jesus.

75. Favor of God, save me from having to decline invitations to gatherings because of stagnancy or backwardness, in the name of Jesus.

76. Favor of God, save me from lack of imagination because of lack, in the name of Jesus.

77. Favor of God, save me from the inability to dream big because of poverty, in the name of Jesus.

78. Favor of God put an end to me letting go off my dreams because there is no money, in the name of Jesus.

79. God's kindness to me guarantees my success in this life, in the name of Jesus.

80. God's benevolence to me ensures that I shall thrive financially, in the name of Jesus.

81. God's generosity to me guarantees that I shall flourish financially, in the name of Jesus.

82. The divine backing of the Lord for me guarantees that I shall make and have abundant money, in the name of Jesus.

83. God's helping hand stretched to me guarantees that I shall profit in business, in the name of Jesus.

84. God's hand of assistance toward me ensures that I will do well financially, in the name of Jesus.

85. Now, I declare that I shall become wealthy and affluent soonest, in the name of Jesus.

86. Milk and honey shall flow into my life, in the name of Jesus.

87. I shall have deep pockets, in the name of Jesus.

88. Loaded bank accounts are my portion as is capital for investment, in the name of Jesus.

89. Financial satisfaction produced by the favor of God is my portion, in the name of Jesus.

90. Thank You everlasting Father for answering my prayers, in Jesus' mighty name, amen.

CHAPTER 31

FAVOR FOR CAREER SUCCESS

**"And let the beauty of the LORD our God be upon us:
and establish thou the work of our hands upon us; yea,
the work of our hands establish thou it."**
— Psalm 90:17 (KJV)

PURPOSE

This prayer session is:

- For achieving career satisfaction
- For obtaining workplace promotions
- For securing better pay
- For overall financial well-being until and into
  retirement

PRAYERS

NOTE: Some of these prayers may not apply to your specific situation. Feel free to skip any which do not.

1. Abba Father, according to Your word, let Your beauty be upon me, in the name of Jesus.

2. My God, according to Your word, be favorable unto me and establish the work of my hands, in the name of Jesus.

3. If I have found grace in Your eyes, O Lord, help me to grow into a person with the ability to manage time in a way that will move me forward, in the name of Jesus.

4. My God, by reason of Your divine favor, give me everything I need to increase the quality of my performance at work, in the name of Jesus.

5. Father, I want to be promoted and paid a higher salary. By reason of Your favor in my life, hold my hand and take me through whatever I need to do or whatever needs to happen in order for my desire to manifest, in the name of Jesus.

6. Holy and True God, help me to become so deep-rooted in my career that I will be rewarded with not only a higher pay but with greater responsibilities and power, in the name of Jesus.

7. O my God, I really desire to become _____ (desired work position) at my workplace. Have compassion on me and let me secure this position, in the name of Jesus.

8. Everlasting Father, if I ever want to move to another company, it would be _____ (desired company). Be merciful unto me and let my desire be established, in the name of Jesus.

9. King of kings, if ever I want to change my field or industry, I would like to secure a job in _____ (desired industry). Have compassion on me and let my desire be established in reality, in the name of Jesus.

10. Lord of lords, I want to have the leaders and stars of my industry as friends. Give me Your favor so that this can become a reality for me, in the name of Jesus.

11. Eternal King, to be respected in my field, I know I need to demonstrate knowledge. Set me up with everything I need to secure all the relevant certifications in my field, in the name of Jesus.

12. Holy Father, I need to get higher formal qualifications. Specifically, I need to get a _____ (qualification e.g. Master's). Let my desire be established, in the name of Jesus.

13. Lord, let my desire to save more of the income I earn be established, in the name of Jesus.

14. Father, help me to cut out wastage and expenses so that I can build up my bank account, in the name of Jesus.

15. Almighty God, I want to become an expert in my workplace and in my field. Anoint me with the knack and the wherewithal to develop great expertise, in the name of Jesus.

16. My Father and my God, the skills that I have may not be enough to take me to the top of my field. Give me the mental and anything else I need to drastically expand my skillset, in the name of Jesus.

17. Lord, let the natural result of my improved knowledge and the consistent application of my skills be recognition and awards at my workplace and in my industry, in the name of Jesus.

18. Elohim, by reason of the recognition and the awards, cause me to become a leader and a positive reference point in my industry, in the name of Jesus.

19. Father, if I have all the skills or abilities in the world but cannot effectively communicate about them or transmit them to others, it may not benefit me much in the long run. Be favorable unto me, Lord, and give me public speaking endowments, in the name of Jesus.

20. Lord, turn me into a person with vast knowledge and who can communicate what I know such that people always understand what I am saying, in the name of Jesus.

21. Jehovah, if I need to become a consultant in the future, bless me with the ability to transmit knowledge in any way that will benefit my clients, in the name of Jesus.

22. Jehovah, let my desire to have my own consulting business be established, in the name of Jesus.

23. My Shepherd, may my consulting business cause a blessed explosion, for good, in my finances, in the name of Jesus.

24. In my current job, O Lord, I do not have a good relationship with _____ (name of colleague). Be gracious unto me, Lord, and let our relationship be repaired, in the name of Jesus.

25. By Your favor, O Lord, reveal unto me how to better relate with my workplace colleagues, in the name of Jesus.

26. Lord, whenever it is requested of me, teach me how to artfully give my view on workplace issues in ways that can never be faulted, in the name of Jesus.

27. By reason of Your favor upon my life, O God, I shall enjoy the obvious favor of my superiors, in the name of Jesus.

28. Have mercy on me, O God, and stream into my consciousness the necessary inspiration to establish a new way of doing things at work for myself and for others, in the name of Jesus.

29. Make me a creator of new standards at work, O God, in the name of Jesus.

30. Lord, bless me such that the team that I am part of will create new and profitable ***products***, in the name of Jesus.

31. Lord, empower me such that I, by myself, will create new and profitable *products* for my employers, in the name of Jesus.

32. Lord, bless me such that the team that I am part of will introduce new and profitable ***services***, in the name of Jesus.

33. Lord, empower me such that I, by myself, will introduce new and profitable services for the benefit of my employers, in the name of Jesus.

34. Great Redeemer, may I never be accused or found guilty of underwork or laziness, in the name of Jesus.

35. Lord God, may I never fall into the trap of overwork and exhaustion, in the name of Jesus.

36. Teach me balance, O Lord, so that I may enjoy lasting satisfaction in my career, in the name of Jesus.

37. Father, let this balance be particularly manifest between my work and my home, in the name of Jesus.

38. Father, let my employers always say that they are satisfied with my output, in the name of Jesus.

39. Father, let my family members also always say that they are happy with me and the time that I spend with them, in the name of Jesus.

40. Holy One of Israel, do not let me be caught in the web of time and forget to plan for my old age. Give me the wisdom to establish a rock solid foundation for my retirement even from now, in the name of Jesus.

41. I declare today: Before I retire from my career, to the glory of Almighty God, I shall become a known brand wherever I work and in my industry, in the name of Jesus.

42. I declare that, by reason of the favor of God upon my life, the brand that I shall establish shall secure for me career portability and income stability, in the name of Jesus.

43. When I am old and enjoying the fruit of a lifetime of good work with my spouse, children and descendants, may I always thank You Father for the favor that You gave to me for my career, in the name of Jesus.

44. Thank You Father God for answering my prayers, in Jesus' mighty name, amen.

CHAPTER 32

FAVOR FOR BUSINESS SUCCESS

**"And let the beauty of the LORD our God be upon us:
and establish thou the work of our hands upon us; yea,
the work of our hands establish thou it."
— Psalm 90:17 (KJV)**

PURPOSE

This prayer session is:

- For the establishment of your business
- For favor with your workers
- For favor with your customers
- For the financial establishment of your family

PRAYERS

NOTE: Some of these prayers may not apply to your specific situation. Feel free to skip any which do not.

1. Jehovah, You are the maker of the universe. If Your beauty comes upon my business, I know it will be established. Make this a reality in my life, in the name of Jesus.

2. Father, I have put my time, blood and sweat into my business, "_____" (name of business). Have mercy and establish _____ (name of business), in the name of Jesus.

3. My God, I know that all human beings have 24 hours every day. I want to make the most of my own 24 hours. Favor me with an uncommon respect for and profitable usage of time everyday, in the name of Jesus.

4. O my Father, I know that success in business requires discipline. Teach me the discipline that I need to secure the prosperity of my business, in the name of Jesus.

5. Favor me, O God, so I can have the resources necessary for improving my online or offline business premises to the taste of my clients, in the name of Jesus.

6. Lord, use Your favor upon my life to help me improve my **product** offerings to be better than the best of my competitors, in the name of Jesus.

7. Father, let Your favor in my life cause me to be able to offer **services** that are better than the best of my competitors, in the name of Jesus.

8. O Mighty God, let Your face shine upon me such that my customers will always be satisfied with my offerings, in the name of Jesus.

9. O God, let Your favor upon me and upon my business cause customers to always return for more, in the name of Jesus.

10. Establish my business, O Lord, by showing me how to increase the speed of my **product** delivery, in the name of Jesus.

11. Establish my business, O Lord, by showing me how to increase the speed of my **service** delivery, in the name of Jesus.

12. My Father and my God, sustain my business by teaching me unique ways to better manage my workers, in the name of Jesus.

13. Lord God, help me to learn the best tone with which to communicate with my staff, in the name of Jesus.

14. Father, make me better at fairly resolving issues that may arise amongst or with my staff, in the name of Jesus.

15. My God, a business is always as strong as the love its workers have for it. Give me favor before my workers so I can win their hearts and their devotion while they work for me, in the name of Jesus.

16. Messiah, have compassion on me. Bless me with whatever I need to remunerate my workers with wages equal to or better than the industry standard, in the name of Jesus.

17. Almighty, bless me with whatever I need to create the right environment for my staff so they can give their best to me and my business, in the name of Jesus.

18. Father, be merciful unto me and my business and let me have highly skilled workers who will be willing to stay with me for reasonable lengths of time, in the name of Jesus.

19. Father, bless me with the knowledge or with someone who has the knowledge of targeted marketing so that I can always reach out to those who need my products and services, in the name of Jesus.

20. May I master or find someone who has mastered the art of advertising in a way that will cause my business to be besieged by customers seeking to buy my products and services, in the name of Jesus.

21. Favor me, O Lord and in addition to my existing customers, let new customers constantly find their way to my business, in the name of Jesus.

22. I receive divine inspiration to create new, quality **products** for the benefit of my customers, in the name of Jesus.

23. I receive divine inspiration to create new, quality **services** for the benefit of my customers, in the name of Jesus.

24. My God, for as long as I shall run my business, let the profit I shall make in one year be vastly greater than that which I made the previous year, in the name of Jesus.

25. Everlasting Father, in addition to whatever my knowledge and experience tells me, reveal to me how to cut unnecessary costs and prevent wastage in my business without reducing the quality of my products or services, in the name of Jesus.

26. King of kings, I hand over all malicious competitors into Your hands. Judge them how You know best, in the name of Jesus.

27. Lord of lords, let all tactics being used by or that will be used by malicious competitors against me fail flatly, in the name of Jesus.

28. I am and shall be the head and not the tail, in the name of Jesus.

29. Ah Lord God, in addition to what my knowledge and experience have taught me, show me how to reach out to my community with benefits that they will love, in the name of Jesus.

30. Father, let me increase in Your favor to such an extent that my customers should love me personally and patronize my business because of the love they have for me, in the name of Jesus.

31. O God, bless me with excellent and trustworthy managers who can keep things running whether I am physically present at the business or not, in the name of Jesus.

32. El Olam, favor me with the financial wherewithal to acquire competitors so I can expand my business significantly, in the name of Jesus.

33. Have compassion on me, O God, and do not let any new and unfair regulation arise that can damage my business, in the name of Jesus.

34. By reason of Your favor upon me, O God, my products and services shall dominate my industry, in the name of Jesus.

35. By reason of Your favor upon me, O God, my customers will become the best advertisers of my products and services, in the name of Jesus.

36. God's favor will see to it that my family shall become established economically by reason of my business, in the name of Jesus.

37. May the favor of God make it such that I can build my business to such a degree that my children will be willing and proud to work with me while I am still there and to continue it after I retire, in the name of Jesus.

38. Thank You O God for Your special favor in answering these prayers of mine, in Jesus' mighty name, amen.

CHAPTER 33

THE TIME FOR DIVINE FAVOR IS NOW!

"Thou shalt arise, and have mercy upon Zion: for the time to favour her, yea, the set time, is come."
— Psalm 102:13 (KJV)

PURPOSE

This prayer session is:

- For quick manifestation of God's divine favor in your life

PRAYERS

1. My Father and my God, throughout this book, I have read and believed and acted and prayed. According to Your word, the time to favor me has come. Unleash Your favor in my life now, in the name of Jesus.

2. O Lord, I am ready for Your favor. The set time to favor me has come. Release Your favor into my life now, in the name of Jesus.

3. O Lord my God, let all my prayers thus far receive answers now, in the name of Jesus.

4. Lord, I do not want Your favor later. Give it to me both now and later, in the name of Jesus.

5. O Lord, You are my God. I do not want Your favor whenever possible. Give it to me now, in the name of Jesus.

6. Lord God of heaven, I do not want Your face to shine upon me at a convenient time. Let it shine on me now, in the name of Jesus.

7. Hear me O Lord, do not send me Your compassion after a delay. Send it to me now, in the name of Jesus.

8. O Lord, I pray, do not let me find favor with you gradually. Let me find favor with You now, in the name of Jesus.

9. O great and awesome God, do not let me find grace in Your sight eventually. Let me find grace in Your sight now, in the name of Jesus.

10. Most High God, do not let my destiny take heavy steps. Let it take quick steps so it can manifest quickly, in the name of Jesus.

11. O my God, have compassion. Do not let the appearance of my glory be sluggish. Let the appearance be hastened, in the name of Jesus.

12. O Lord, I trust in You. Do not let me obtain Your favor finally. Let me obtain it now, in the name of Jesus.

13. O God, life is short and You have given me a program to fulfill here on earth. Have mercy and give me Your favor now, in the name of Jesus.

14. Rise up for my sake, O Lord, and let me begin to increase in favor with You now, in the name of Jesus.

15. God's kindness will not be shown to me sometime in the by and by. No, it will be shown to me today, in the name of Jesus.

16. God's grace will not be shown to me in due course only. I will benefit it from it both now and in due course, in the name of Jesus.

17. God will not be benevolent to me at a future time only. He will be benevolent to me now and in the future, in the name of Jesus.

18. I will not become the object of God's goodwill after a while. I will become the object of His goodwill now, in the name of Jesus.

19. God will not be generous to me one of these days. According to His word, He will be generous to me now and on other days, in the name of Jesus.

20. God will not stretch His helping hand to me in the long run. He will stretch it to me both now and in the long run, in the name of Jesus.

21. The favor of the Lord is causing me to **grow** now, in the name of Jesus

22. The favor of the Lord is causing me to **be secure** now, in the name of Jesus

23. The favor of the Lord is causing me to **develop** now, in the name of Jesus

24. The favor of the Lord is setting me up for success now, in the name of Jesus

25. The favor of the Lord is backing me up now, in the name of Jesus

26. The favor of the Lord is encouraging me now, in the name of Jesus

27. The favor of the Lord is supporting me now, in the name of Jesus

28. The favor of the Lord is sustaining me now, in the name of Jesus

29. The favor of the Lord is helping me achieve now, in the name of Jesus

30. The favor of the Lord is helping me perform now, in the name of Jesus

31. The favor of the Lord is helping me execute now, in the name of Jesus

32. The favor of the Lord is guiding me now, in the name of Jesus

33. The favor of the Lord is instructing me now, in the name of Jesus

34. The favor of the Lord is getting things approved for me now, in the name of Jesus

35. By reason of the favor of the Lord, I am firmly established in this life, in the name of Jesus.

36. Thank You Almighty God for answering all my prayers in this book, in Jesus' mighty name, amen.

DOWNLOAD YOUR BONUS

FAVOR
FOR
UNMERITED
ASSISTANCE

Once again, thank you for getting "Pray Your Way Into Divine Favor" (Exhaustive Edition)

Use the link on this page to access the accompanying bonus chapter *"Favor for Unmerited Assistance"* for free.

USE THE LINK BELOW TO DOWNLOAD YOUR BONUS CHAPTER NOW.

HTTPS://SUPPORT.PRAYERDB.COM/?FF_LANDING=75

Printed in Great Britain
by Amazon